Airplane Reading

Airplane Reading

Edited by Christopher Schaberg
& Mark Yakich

Winchester, UK
Washington, USA

First published by Zero Books, 2016
Zero Books is an imprint of John Hunt Publishing Ltd., Laurel House, Station Approach,
Alresford, Hants, SO24 9JH, UK
office1@jhpbooks.net
www.johnhuntpublishing.com
www.zero-books.net

For distributor details and how to order please visit the 'Ordering' section on our website.

Text copyright: Christopher Schaberg & Mark Yakich 2015

ISBN: 978 1 78279 818 7
Library of Congress Control Number: 2015958684

A CIP catalogue record for this book is available from the British Library.

Design: Stuart Davies

Printed in the USA by Edwards Brothers Malloy

We operate a distinctive and ethical publishing philosophy in all
areas of our business, from our global network of authors to
production and worldwide distribution.

CONTENTS

The airplane has unveiled to us the true face of the earth.

—Antoine de Saint-Exupery

You haven't seen a tree until you've seen its shadow from the sky.

—Amelia Earhart

Introduction

Christopher Schaberg & Mark Yakich

And here we are again, heading to the airport. One of us is filled with a kind of ongoing delight, and one of us has just eaten a banana and Xanax for breakfast. In this forest-green Subaru Forester, we're not exactly commuting to work, and yet perhaps we are.

It was six years ago when we met each other for the first time—at an airport's curbside—and only weeks thereafter we began writing collaborative pieces about air travel. Since then, airliners have been lost and found, been grounded and re-approved for safe flight, shot out of the sky with ballistic missiles, and taken off and landed, day in and day out, a thousand unremarkable flights each hour, on and on.

In that time—the days and years—we've gathered hundreds of air-travel stories, first on our website airplanereading.org and now a selected number in this book. These stories range from the humorous and odd to serious and sad, spanning the spectrum of emotions and experiences associated with flight.

Our book does not express a unified interpretation of air travel, but rather seeks to reflect a broad swath of people's observations and reflections: of sitting around the airport, being in the air, waiting for takeoff or landing. Yet there is something apocryphal about this book, too. The perspectives shared in this book are not uniformly upbeat; they are frequently wary of this whole enterprise called flight. At the same time, there are moments of sublimity and enlightenment as our contributors ponder airborne existence.

The stories in this book are by regular travelers, frequent flyers, and occasional aviators.

And who are we?

One of us used to work at an airport and has written articles and books about the culture of flight. The other used to live abroad, regularly flying across continents, and slowly but steadily developed a fear of flying, along with a penchant for poetry.

And where are we now, as we write the introduction to this book?

We've arrived at the Lakefront Airport on the east side of New Orleans. There's virtually no security, no problem parking, and almost no one around. As part of post-Katrina rebuilding, this airport has been restored—just this year—to its original 1930s glamour. On the outside, workers have removed 1960s concrete structures (placed there so that the building could be used as a nuclear-fallout shelter) to reveal a stunning art-deco facade; and on the inside, an artist is in the process of restoring seven paintings by Xavier Gonzalez that depict the early age of flight.

Turns out the restaurant and bar is closed on Mondays, but a woman in black sweats let us into the café and here we are sitting at a two-top with no one else in sight. Small private aircraft taxi, take off, and land out on the runway, mere feet away from us as we write. It is strange to be here by ourselves. It's like being at a museum in the off-hours. But it is only mid-morning, and some kind of small plane sits nearby, with "United States of America" emblazoned on its fuselage, and we're speculating about whether it's FBI, CIA, or secret service. There's no particular reason for our speculation, except that we're at the airport and, if nothing else, airports still seem to be one of the few places left to enjoy undirected daydreaming.

Another jet sits nearby, and this one, a Gulfstream 6, dons a legible tail number: N305KN—but further information about this plane is blocked when googled. One of us remarks that this would be the airport, as opposed to Louis Armstrong International, for shady business deals and corresponding clandestine flight plans. If the airport feels charmingly dated, it also lends itself to new airplanes potentially charged with intrigue and espionage. Seemingly on cue, a sleek-looking Avanti Evo now taxis by, as if right off the set of *Miami Vice*.

One of us is staring off into the distance, thinking about the perfectly trimmed grass between the runways and how ideal it would be to install a soccer pitch right there. Or better yet, what a lovely place for a cemetery. What would it be like to be buried alongside a runway, underneath wide-open, tree-less skies? And what would it be like to land amid rows of headstones and above-ground mausoleums?

The other one of us is snapping pictures of an old Eastern Air Lines air stair, whose tarnished gray metal and defunct logo appear at odds with the gleaming white Gulfstream fifty feet away. Decades of disparate aviation endeavors slice across the tarmac here, and we sit nearby, neutral observers—as if.

Across the runway rest two WWII bombers: one a B-17 "Flying Fortress," the other a B-29 "Superfortress." A good portion of the airborne violence of the twentieth century— symbolically if not literally speaking—sitting calmly in an autumn rain, the leftovers of Hurricane Patricia which slammed into Mexico a few days ago. We each noticed over the weekend when one of these planes circled over the city, its unfamiliar drone thundering above—looking now, we learn that there was an "Air Power Expo" here over the weekend. This B-29 is named "FIFI"—the last of the B-29s still flying. The Lakefront Airport is a strange whorl of aviation's decades—still in process, patterns vaguely the same.

Being in this airport is like inhabiting the whole history of flight. Or is that the case with being in any airport, staring out at a runway horizon? The expanse reaching from here to there has never really changed all that much.

A swarthy bank of gray clouds is descending on us, barreling over Lake Pontchartrain. One of us is happy that we don't have to fly today; the other wouldn't mind a brief trip aboard one of the old bombers, as civilians could have purchased over this past weekend at the expo for the cool price of $1500.

We only came out here to get a certain distance from our daily lives, to harness some of the imagination that sparks airplane reading. It's about wonder, history, beauty, existential dread, even death—and it's about how flight can swoop into our lives, and depart just as easily.

It's lunchtime, and now three separate couples and families have poked their heads into the cafe. "Anybody here?" From around the corner, stationed at our table, we tell them: "No, sorry, we're closed today—open Tuesday through Sunday." It's seamless. They think we work here. And we do, in a curious way.

We've somehow arrived at a destination, albeit at the wrong time. Or, the right time for us—but somehow at odds with the intended experience of this place. This encapsulates our airplane-reading journey: always seeing airport and airplane things somewhat aslant.

We plan to stay the rest of the day, standing on the observation deck—weather permitting, the rain has let up, for now—looking out over the runway, watching takeoffs and landings, imagining each plane's stories, including them in our own, this archaeology of airplane reading.

The Work of Gravity

Roxane Gay

When I was a child, the people who smoked at the back of the airplane were so sophisticated. They sat in the last four or five or six rows, lounging in a gray cloud of smoke that always drifted toward the front of the plane. Every section on the airplane in those days was, really, a smoking section. My mother has a strong aversion to cigarette smoke and anytime we were on a plane, which was often, she would frown and grumble about the rudeness of smokers. She'd cough, loudly, and sigh.

Me, I loved to turn around and watch the smokers—men in suits, sitting with their long legs in the aisle, women with their lipstick staining the filter tip. I studied the different ways the smokers exhaled—through the nose in twin streams of gray, in a firm line from the lips, in carefully measured circles, sloppy bursts of air. I especially enjoyed how the smokers ashed their cigarettes into the little ashtray in the armrest, such a smart invention. I've always been fond of things that are more complicated than they first seem.

There is a moment when the airplane first leaves the ground and gravity starts to do its work. It presses down on you and your body is pulled to the back of your seat and you nearly can't move. That moment, terrifying and exhilarating, is one of the purest reminders that there is so much beyond our understanding.

I went to boarding school at thirteen years old. My parents moved around a lot because of my father's job. I mostly enjoyed always getting to know a new place, and I loved my family, but I wanted to go to the same high school for four years. I had seen enough movies to know high school would be the most important time of my life. I also wanted to run away. Junior high had been rough in ways I did not think were possible. I wanted to run away from the boy across the street, the boy I loved, the boy I thought was my friend only to learn he was anything but, the boy who took my love and tore it up and shared it with other boys he had no business sharing it with. When you run away, you always think you're running toward something better. We need to believe we're running toward something better to give us the courage to leave. I needed to believe I was running toward something better, a place where no one knew anything about me. I got on a plane, alone, and a flight attendant handed me a plastic set of wings. I held them in my hand and told her, "I am not a child." She patted my shoulder and escorted me to my seat. After the plane took off, I exhaled and smiled. I turned around to look at the smokers, sophisticated and cool, inhaling and exhaling, making it hard for anyone to breathe from within their shroud of smoke. It was a small price to pay. Of course I thought I was free.

When I flew home on breaks, I generally traveled on Eastern Air lines. They had the prettiest planes—a shiny chrome tube with a line of sky blue and a line of darker blue stretched along the fuselage. On my way home, I'd wait for my flight, my stomach knotted with all my worries. On the way back to school from wherever, I'd wait for my flight, my stomach knotted with all my worries. Throughout my teens, I was a mass of raw nerves. On the plane, though, particularly during the late flights, with the cabin dark save for a few beams of overhead light, I always felt perfectly calm, surrounded by strangers and the loud silence of a quiet airplane.

I started smoking when I was fifteen—picked up the habit at summer camp where the counselors amused themselves by corrupting the older campers once they put the younger campers to bed. I always felt cool when I smoked, and it relaxed me, the ritual of it. The knots in my stomach slowly unraveled when I lit a fresh cigarette. I smoked a lot.

I was only able to smoke on airplanes for less than a year

before the government banned smoking on all domestic flights shorter than six hours. Once the plane took off, after that terrifying, exhilarating moment when gravity pressed down on me, I'd stare at the console overhead, tapping my fingers against the armrest, waiting, waiting, waiting for the NO SMOKING light to disappear. When it did, everyone in the smoking section worked in concert, alone but together, cigarettes at the ready, the flick of the lighter, the deep inhale, holding the sweet smoke in our chests, the collective exhale.

Frequent Flight

Ian Bogost

I will fly more than 200,000 miles this year. It routinizes, like an extended commute. The suburbanite knows every moment of the drive: on-ramp, lane-change, morning-show, cup-holder. I'm like that, but on a global vector: freeway, parking lot, door S-3, South security checkpoint, wallet, shoes, laptop, zip-lock, escalator, train, SkyClub, jetway, seat, jacket, bourbon, nap, tarmac, sky, sky, sky.

We frequent flyers are the wizened, aged elders to the leisure-traveler cherubim. Our vacant glances tousle your collective heads. We are the aviary aristocracy. Coach is a curious memory, a favela from a forgotten youth. An Atlantis that sank into the fuselage.

We can go ten days in the 18" roll-aboard. With three suits. With an umbrella. We know the order of the fare classes. We know how to Q-UP. We do not complain about delays or IROPs. We were going to be on a plane anyway, or a hotel, or a conference center. We are unfazed, save by the fazed whose perturbedness perturbs us. We have broken the wild stallion whose nostrils flare with the steam of tarmac. We have resisted the siren whose bright blueness stares us down through oval portals.

"Frequent flyer" is misleading. So frequent is the frequency that the ground becomes the figure, the sky the ground. We are the sometimes-grounded.

We have eaten all the meals they don't serve you. Domestic: check the flight number. Orders are taken from the front on even flights, back on odd; we choose seats early to avoid the wet sandwich. International: we've already eaten the filet of beef with demi-glace sauce, the curried chicken, even the pan-seared cod.

Even the cold plate of roast beef and gravlax. We're considering the strozzapreti. Not from desperation nor vegetarianism, but just from ennui. Eventually we stop ordering anything. A flying problem is the opposite of a drinking problem: it starts when you lose interest in the free booze.

Like grandfathers or autistic people, we do not speak except to remark about those who violate the custom. Social rites develop only around circumstances of unpredictable exception. The window seat is a two-hour renewable contract not to use the lavatory. Or the primary ritual: on the 752 or the 763, will the jetway dock at the first or the second door? We stoop and crane to see, looking out the windows for the first time. Then we all turn accordingly, silently, like synchronized swimmers with iPhones. Like migrating birds with elite-status wing tags.

Eventually, the flights seep out from the planes, from the airports like mercury. Slowly they cover things. We do not own toiletries larger than 3.4oz. Every jacket pocket contains an old boarding pass. We long since gave up bringing home souvenirs in favor of airplane cookies. Our children hug us and ask, "Did you bring airplane cookies?" Of course we did. Every jacket pocket contains an old boarding pass and a Biscoff cookie. Sometimes we eat one, like a Proustian madeleine. The cinnamon sweetness tastes like cabin pressure and pale loneliness and turbofan hum.

There are amateurs and there are experts. Or better, there are initiates and there are the initiated. The flipside of strangeness is habituation. It's true in all things. The dentist for whom every day is a day at the dentist's. The pastry chef who pipes special occasions into indistinction. The wary schoolboy who becomes the weary schoolboy. The traveler who becomes the frequent flyer.

Why I Love to Fly

Pam Houston

It is 8:00 AM on a Sunday morning in September, and I am down in the East Jesus section of the Denver International Airport where all the smallest United Express flights come and go. I have already flown once today—Casper to Denver, another puddle-jumper—and watched the sunrise over the western reaches of the Great Plains, the light glinting off dozens of potholes in south-eastern Wyoming's moonscape topography.

They announce our flight, which, down in this modified trailer park of a terminal means a guy shouts "Durango?" in my general direction and waves his arm. I cross the tarmac and climb the stairs into the little Embraer 145, and take seat 1A. Even though this is an all-Economy aircraft, I am entitled to board first and sit in seat 1A because I fly more than a hundred-thousand miles on United each year. This last year, somewhere over Greenland on my way back from Athens, I crossed the million-mile mark (lifetime) with United, and it was everything I'd dreamed it would be. They announced my name over the loudspeaker, gave me a bottle of pretty good Australian Shiraz, and the pilot (who was not, unfortunately, Sam Elliott) came out of the cockpit, sat down with me and shook my hand.

As I get myself settled in seat 1A, Kool and the Gang's "Celebration" is cranking—and I mean cranking—over the PA system, and the young male flight attendant, whose name tag says Matt, is doing a modified version of the Swim in the tiny galley that on the Embraer is right across the aisle from seat 1A.

"We're going zip-lining when we get to Durango!" he shouts to me over the music with so much enthusiasm that for a second I think he means we are going zip-lining, me and him, or perhaps all 18 of us on the flight, but then the pilot leans out of the cockpit to slap Matt a high-five and I realize "we" in this case means the three-man crew.

"Cool," I say, as the end of "Celebration" bleeds into the first few notes of Tavares' "Heaven Must Be Missing an Angel."

"Can you imagine?" he says, "how it's gonna be up there this week with all of the trees flaming out?"

"This flight," I say, "ought to be pretty outrageous too."

It's the third week of September in Colorado and the giant Aspen groves (the world's largest living organism, thousands of acres of trees all connected by their roots) that cover the western half of the state will be lighting up in swathes of color the size of football fields; green to yellow, yellow to gold, gold to vermilion. Our flight, which must be one of the most spectacular commercial flights in all the world, will climb through Rocky Mountain National Park, cross Arapaho Basin, catch the north end of the Collegiate Range and Independence Pass just east of the town of Aspen. Then, most dramatically of all, we will traverse the high San Juans near the melting rum-raisin ice-cream cone of Uncompaghre Peak, before we begin our final descent into Durango.

When Gloria Gaynor starts singing "I Will Survive," and Matt turns it up one notch further and uses his demonstration seatbelt as a lip-syncing microphone, it proves too much for the older couple over my left shoulder in seats 3B and C. They start making faces and sounds of displeasure, which I watch Matt take note of and choose to ignore.

"Good morning ladies and gentleman!" his voice booms over the booming music. "It's Disco Sunday on United Airlines and we are so happy you are here to experience what may turn out to be the most beautiful airline flight in the history of the Universe."

I glance back at *Mr. and Mrs. No Fun At All* and see that they are deciding whether or not to relax into Matt's routine and for everyone's sake I encourage them with my eyes.

"Ladies and gentlemen," Matt says, "you are not going to believe this, but a couple of hours ago, before the sun had even started to rise, one of United's finest mechanics, John Baker, was lying under this airplane with oil and anti-freeze and a lot of other toxic fluids dripping right into his ear, and it is to him we owe our impending on-time departure, and because of him we WILL survive today, along with the delightful Ms. Gaynor."

We get only halfway through "Play That Funky Music, White Boy," before Matt has to turn down the music and play the safety-demonstration tape.

When we sail past Longs Peak the west wind is blowing the early snow off the top into a cloud shaped just like a spinnaker, and I spot three sapphire-blue glacial tarns on the mountain's various flanks. On the eastern approach to Independence Pass a herd of elk 200-strong is running across a high-mountain meadow, the tundra beneath their hooves a deep red and gold. And when we leave Crested Butte behind under the wing and make the big turn southward, Slumgullion Pass is on our right and Baldy Cinco is on our left and as we skate down the south side of Spring Creek Pass, I am all of a sudden looking at my very own valley.

"Matt!" I say. "Come here, come here, come here!" He crouches in the aisle so he can see out my window. "That's my house!"

"Really?"

"Yes, that one all by itself out there, down at the end of the valley."

"Near that little clump of pine trees?"

"Yes!"

"You live there?"

"YES!"

"What in the world," he asks, "do you do out here?"

And it's true, no matter which window we look out we see only vast pine and aspen forest, a few snow dusted 14,000-foot peaks, the broad snaking valley of the upper Rio Grande, a very occasional cluster of weathered buildings, and very little, it seems, to do.

"I write books," I say. "Novels."

"You're shitting me."

"No," I say, "in fact, the new one is called *Contents May Have Shifted*."

"It is not," he says.

"It is!" I say. "I named it after you...you know...in a way."

"Ladies and gentlemen," Matt says into his microphone, "you are never going to believe this..."

As we hang a deep left over Beartown and follow the path of the Silverton railroad toward Durango, Matt makes an announcement over the PA system about my forthcoming novel.

It goes without saying that the enthusiasm is entirely his.

Flying Au Naturale

Connie Porter

Reading the *New York Times* this past August, I was drawn to the headline, "With Hair Pat Downs, Complaints Of Racial Bias." Two African-American women, Timery Shante Nance and Laura Adele, were both stopped by TSA agents this summer.

Ms. Nance was stopped at the security checkpoint in the San Antonio airport, Ms. Adele in the Seattle-Tacoma airport. Though neither woman had set off any alarms, both were stopped and TSA agents felt they needed to pat down their hair—their natural hair.

One might argue that these are isolated incidents. Since we live in a post-9/11 world, for matters of security, we must allow the TSA and its employees to set up procedures that assure that we are all safe. If the TSA deems natural hair on black women as a potential threat to the nation, who is to say it isn't?

Being a black woman who wears her hair natural, I know that black women's natural hair can be big and thick, so wound in dark clouds of twists and braids that maybe it looks to an untrained eye as if we are hiding something in our hair. But after clearing metal detectors, what exactly is suspect? What could we be hiding in our hair?

Is the baby Moses asleep in our reedy dreads? Is there a smuggled lorikeet nesting in our braids?

Perhaps our hair itself is suspect. Terrifying. *That* hair. Unbent by curling irons, untouched by relaxers, straightening combs, or flat irons. Our natural hair has the profile of a potential terrorist and has made it onto the "Do Search" list.

The "Do Search" list isn't new. It existed pre-9/11. I know because I was on it when I began flying *au naturale*.

Two years before then, I was happy to be nappy, flying

frequently to promote a novel and children's books I had published. If you were behind me, you wouldn't have noticed me, a small dark-skinned black woman with an Eddie Bauer briefcase, a bottle of water, and a head full of natural twists. You wouldn't have known that I was a one-woman delay. My stop would've seemed random to you. Except that it wasn't. Virtually every time I stepped a foot through security, I was pulled aside for additional screening. Like Ms. Nance and Ms. Adele, I passed through the metal detector, my bag made it through the x-ray — then I was pulled aside.

It became frustrating, and more, something that angered me. I began observing that during these checks, I was the only one pulled out of line, or if someone else was, it was because he or she had set off the alarm.

When I told one of my brothers about it, he said, "They probably think you're a drug courier."

I laughed at the sheer ridiculousness of the thought. "Me!? I have never done an illegal drug in my life."

My dark-skin and nappy-hair twice-monthly flights were adding up to the screeners — not as me being an author, but a drug mule.

When I was in college, I used to get asked by male students of the African Diaspora where I was from — Jamaica, Haiti, Ethiopia, Cameroon? One young man didn't believe me when I told him that I was from Lackawanna, New York, and that my parents were from Alabama. My answer angered him. He insisted I was a Jamaican, as was he. Worse, I was a self-hating Jamaican whose family had instructed me to lie about my heritage. That was his theory, and he was sticking to it.

We all are capable of formulating theories, and sticking to them. They don't have to be based in fact, just our beliefs. In college, I didn't realize I *was* the face of the Diaspora, the embodiment of all the women they thought I was, and who I knew I was. I was from Africa, east and west, a sojourner through the islands of the Caribbean, a daughter of the Second Great Migration of African-Americans from South to North.

Perhaps Chaka said it best—to these young men, I was "every woman."

To airport security, I was *that* woman. The one to be stopped and searched. The one who was suspect. A long-lost daughter whose lineage crossed through Kush—was I carrying Kush now, perhaps, in my hair?

With a growing intolerance of my "random" searches, I informed my mother that the next time I was stopped, I was flying *au naturale*: I would jump on the belt at security and strip. Being a well-raised, Southern woman of a certain age, she said, "Well, you wouldn't want to do that."

I didn't do that; instead, the very next time I flew and was stopped, I confronted the screener who stopped me and asked why I was being stopped.

"Ma'am this is a random check," he assured me as he swabbed my briefcase.

"No, this isn't. As a matter of fact, you are the same agent who stopped me the last time I flew."

"No I wasn't," he insisted.

"Yes, you are, and you have stopped me before." This is when I assured him. "You may check thousands of passengers, and don't remember them. I remember you, and I want your full name. I'm reporting you."

He refused to give me his full name, but that didn't matter. I reported him anyway, wrote a letter of complaint to his employer. I never received a reply.

I was still stopped, searched, and had my bag swabbed. I became stoic, feeling as though I had at least said my piece.

When 9/11 happened, and airport security was raised to code ridiculous, I wondered how much had been missed by screeners leading up to that fateful day. Who had they missed, what had they missed while believing some theory about the threat level of my hair? And now, while the *au naturale* hair of black women has taken on a new and heightened threat level of its own, who is breezing past them? Unsuspected, unsearched, sleek-haired and dressed to kill.

Surviving the Unabomber

Arthur Plotnik

I was forty-two when the American Airlines aircraft I'd boarded in Chicago was set to explode in midair.

Beneath me, in the baggage hold, was a live bomb shipped by Theodore Kaczynski, a.k.a. the Unabomber. As we headed toward Washington, D. C., his device ignited a powerful mix of explosive chemicals that somehow failed to incinerate me and seventy-seven others on the plane.

This was November 15, 1979. Miraculous—or lucky—as our survival was, I have never thought of it as the defining event of my life; in fact, I've thought of it surprisingly little as other issues have occupied me over the decades. But now as every day brings ghastly news of bomb casualties—of so many unfolding lives blasted into the void—the heft of my own still-flowering life feels almost unnatural.

I had everything to live for the day I boarded Flight 444 and sat unknowingly above the bomb. My two daughters were just pre-teens; my career as an editor and journalist was flourishing. I'd left a troubled life in New York for a fresh start in Chicago. Divorced, I was enjoying new relationships, developing enlightened attitudes for a second time around.

Meanwhile, Kaczynski was a man who, midway through life's journey, had entered a dark forest and lost his way out. From Chicago and then a cramped cabin in Montana, he was scheming to avenge the perceived evils of technology through symbolic maimings and killings. Before he was captured in 1996, his mail bombs would murder three and injure some twenty-eight.

Early on, he sought to make an emphatic statement by exploding an airliner in mid-flight. He fashioned a bomb out of batteries, a barometer, and enough incendiary chemicals to convert me and my fellow passengers into a tropospheric ball of fire. He packed the bomb in a wooden box, which he then shipped airmail from a Chicago suburb.

It ended up as postal baggage on our flight out of O'Hare. We were bound for Washington National Airport (now Reagan National Airport). According to FBI reports, Kaczynski's homemade altimeter cued the ignition device at 34,500 feet. We should have all died.

His device ignited all right. We heard a thud; acrid smoke streamed from below and choked the cabin. No one knew what had happened, but we were told to don the released oxygen masks and assume crash positions while the pilots raced for Washington's Dulles Airport, some twenty-five minutes away.

Those minutes went by in uncanny silence. With heads nested in folded arms, passengers seemed to be forestalling catastrophe by force of stillness, willing the plane to safety before smoke asphyxiated us or flames reached the fuel tanks. But no doubt the silent thoughts were as varied as the passengers' makeups. Prayers. Anguish. Terror. In my own mind, a soul-sickening flash of mortality shaped itself into a dark mantra: *This is the unspeakable thing that can't be happening, that happens only to others, that we believe will not happen to us—but here it is happening. It IS happening.* I uttered "agnostic-in-a-foxhole" prayers. I thought of my children.

We made it to Dulles—with an abrupt landing that rocketed unfixed objects toward the front. I scrambled through the plane's rear exit and ran with other passengers along the runway past ambulances and fire trucks, ran with the giddiness of being alive. *It still only happens to others. It doesn't happen to me!*

The resonance of mortal fear, the introspection that might have come from a few quiet days was dispelled by journalistic duties and impulses: *Get pictures of the plane and people being treated for smoke inhalation; call in a news tip; get yourself to the convention you're here to cover...*

My giddiness carried over to a brief interview that afternoon on Washington's NBC-TV, which fed my talking head to the national evening news. "Scary," I said, giggling.

Seasons passed before I learned that the muted fire, far from arising from some accidental cause, was connected to the Unabomber. Years went by before smaller details were unveiled: How Kaczynski's package bore a Frederick Douglass stamp and one captioned, "America's light fueled by truth and reason." How he mewled over the cost of the bomb's materials; how he packed a 64-ounce juice can with pyrotechnic chemicals which seem to have burned, but—for reasons still unknown to me—failed to blow.

My life did flower. I worked with words, advanced the cause of libraries—a happy career. I wrote and still write with gratifying results. I've been joyously remarried for over a quarter century. My family enriches my life. My days are full.

But sometimes, when lives are snatched from the latest bomb victims, I'm prompted to seek meaning in my own escape from annihilation. Many of us survive close calls in this hazardous world. Is there a destiny or revelation at play? Are we special? What is it we've been saved to do?

I seek meaning, but come up short.

Survival doesn't anoint me as saint or world-saver. I don't feel chosen or special, or bound to some grand mission. That's TV stuff—or the delusions that sometimes drive unabombers and "martyrs" who blow up children. No, I'm satisfied to be honoring the miracle of life by moving through its luminescence as peacefully, cheerfully, and long as possible. Someone has to be there—people like you and me—to keep the light on. Whether we're enabled to do so by luck or providence, I don't know.

If any epiphany came out of my survival it was when my uncle, a droll California attorney, saw me on NBC that evening and reported, "You were good until you giggled." He had it backward. I was good *when* I giggled, for all the madmen to see.

Excuse Me

Priscila Uppal

Good morning. Good afternoon. Would you mind trading seats, I have a fear of windows. I have long legs. I have a touch of diarrhea. I have to walk every twenty minutes to prevent blood clots. What are you reading? Is it good? I read a review of something or other, a week or so ago, in the *Times* or the *Post*. I wish I could read on a plane. I wish I liked reading. Can I borrow the in-flight magazine? Is there a survey? I like surveys, don't you? Do you like my hair like this—I'm trying something new. I once did a survey and found out that I have an anxiety disorder. That's how it was diagnosed. I sometimes like to refresh myself on the safety procedures. Every life vest has a different pull. How are we supposed to choose our meals if we can't see pictures of the food? I like the look of this chicken wrap. The licorice packaging is happy and bright, I'll have that. What are you going to have? Just don't order peanuts. I'm allergic. I could die. They shouldn't serve nut products on planes. I don't know why they haven't caught up to the times. Is that wrap gluten-free? I also have an allergy to root vegetables. Do you have any allergies? I have an EpiPen on hand, but you never know when some asshole is going to pull out a peanut-butter-and-jelly sandwich or a Mars Bar or something even after the flight crew has made several announcements. You never know who speaks English any more. Not even from their clothes or the screens on their cell phones. You used to know when people read books. I wish I could read on a plane. I wish I liked reading. You seem to like reading. Are you a teacher? Why are you underlining? Are you taking a test? I'm going to take a scuba-diving test. An Indian cooking course. A serial-killers tour. A biochemistry degree. Do you think I'm making a mistake? Degrees seem useless nowadays. Most of my classmates who graduated last year couldn't find jobs. Can you tell me how to find a job? How did you find your job? Do you like my hair like this—it's hard to tell in the tiny washroom? Did you know someone or did you work hard? Where are you from? I'm not from here either. I'm from the coast. I'm from over the pond. I'm from a small town that you'll miss if you fart. I can't wait to land and put on my bikini. My snowboard. My semi-automatic machine gun. I can't wait to meet this guy I met on the Internet. My birth mother. My high-school sweetheart after thirty years. My new Corvette. We're getting married. Beach wedding. Ski-resort wedding. Underwater wedding. Shotgun wedding. That's my dress taking up the entire overhead. Do you think I'm making a mistake? I fell in love with his eyes. His accent. His sense of humor. Her reckless nature. Her legs. Her need to save fragile things. Funeral. Heart attack. Diabetes. Aneurism. Freak amusement-park accident. Cancer. Cancer. Fucking cancer. Do you have a dog? A cat? A parrot? I have ferrets. You take them on the plane like other pets. I have an emotional-support dog. I can take my dog anywhere because if you need an emotional-support dog you have a disability and under the law you must be treated as someone with a disability whose disability aid is a dog. Do you have any disabilities? I wish I had more Pringles. More hair. Do you like my hair like this—I think this is the winner, don't you? More money. More pairs of underwear in my suitcase. More friends. More choices of airlines. More time to sleep. More sleeping pills. More of everything. I regret that. Not speaking to my father for nearly twenty years. Not taking that train along the Rockies. Becoming a dentist instead of a massage therapist. Quitting guitar. Thinking my kids would one day take care of me. My son is addicted to everything. Alcohol. Pot. Porn. Video games. Cat videos. Do you think I made a mistake? I don't like turbulence. I suppose no one does, but I always look around and see people who don't seem to care that the plane is shaking. Eating pretzels. Eating beef jerky. Hummus. Watching an action flick. Comedy. I like watching movies on the plane, but not when there's turbulence. When there's turbulence, all I can do is think to myself, the plane is designed not to crack. The pilot doesn't want to die today. Enjoy the ride. ETA. You don't seem to like turbulence either. At least you can read on a plane. I wish I could read on a plane. What are you reading? One day, I'm going to write a book about my life. It's not easy being a district attorney. It's not easy being a bus driver. It's not easy being a mother of five. It's not easy being mayor, even of a small town. Do you mind turning your light off? I'm going to try to catch a few zzzs. I have another ten-hour flight after this one. I need to replenish my energy before engaging with my in-laws. I've read that book. Interesting. Confusing. Disappointing. It reminded me of a movie I saw last year that had that great actor in it. Nice cover. I like your hair—how do you do that? Would you mind handing me my laptop case? My purse. My umbrella. My duty-free. My customs card. Flights always last one hour past your tolerance point, ever notice that? Can't wait to smell that salty air. Corn dogs. Croissants. Cologne. You can always tell the worth of a pilot by the landing. Can I squeeze past you—I'm in a hurry. Oh, here, you dropped your book. Good luck.

Holding Pattern

Ander Monson

United Airlines flight 5437, Tucson to Denver, 5:15 a.m.
Seat 10D, backseat library.

Not for lending, these volumes, *SkyWest* magazine, with a
feature on "Michigan: Keweenaw Peninsula," my home whether
or not I'd like to claim it. These things claim us: the winter crush,
the lack of touch for weeks, a conversationless month so silent
that one late night I sojourned, unintentional monk, to the
Walmart just to catch a human voice. It fell away soon enough,
brief drift into the cashier's use of CHANT (Customers Have a
Name Too, through which they are instructed to address the
customer by name if the customer presents a card or check), then
my Chinese junk stowed safely in the car in dolphin-throttling
plastic sacks, as if the night had meant to say this long silence is
a sentence diagrammed for you and you alone.

This library is small, meant for me alone, the collection
limited. The CRJ700 Passenger Safety card, there to stay, beside
the point, as we all know, since all we'll be is teeth and Great
Lake vapor—name of a new smokeless cigarette—when we go
down in flame and last-question death mask, but we kowtow to
ritual, pretend to pay attention, just like in school. We got good
at that, the darkening, the silence, tuning out this world, tuning

into another, like cracking an egg and finding in its place another egg but this one filled with glowing something special, and worthy of our hallowed study, our days counting down in study hall to the end of winter.

I study *Hemispheres* from Continental Airlines, crossword only partly done, of course. 37 across, "a book of maps," five letters— they got this one, "atlas," and this mag is too an atlas: here's where we fly, you and Continental Airlines and possibly the hand of god, the clean circular routes to suggest dimension. But for 91, three letters, "forest female," I think they must mean *elf*? But that's crap as any reader knows: elves can too be male or perhaps like always I am up the wrong tree chasing the wrong forest female into greenery from which I will not emerge unscathed. Maybe *sylph* or *dryad* but overlettered, likely too obscure D&D for this. Fox, instead? Or the vixen version, tracks of male and female criss-crossing exes in snow.

43 across, four letters for "excited," good news, they got "agog," but that was it.

A few bits missing: piece of map, torn out as perhaps a scrap of paper or to house gum past-pulverized and geocached for another finder. Knowing that we're allowed to take the magazines home, I do, but the safety-information card's the real prize. I stole dozens for my collection in years past, pleased with the iconography, the odd illustration decisions. I envisioned later planes going down, the crowd, once bored, scrapping for a card, a crutch, a written revelation to clutch into the blur of their final moments. Traveling alone, do you choose another heart's to hold? Does it matter whose? Is it the one who most looks like the one you love? The one you had eyes for on this flight, even if these flirtatious semaphors never crest because where is there to go?

Two barf bags, one unmarked, the other "For Motion Discomfort / Or Baby Diaper Disposal." For deposit, either way. No need to return. I fill mine with snacks. And put it back. A surprise for someone sore-backed, weary, weepy.

I write inappropriate mash notes on napkins on planes and in airports and leave them for another future lover. Start emails I have to then delete and will fear later I had sent them unredacted. An anonymous space makes us bold. We can hold so few, and only briefly.

Take Flight

Chelsey Johnson

I have always led parallel lives, as if one were not enough. Some people do this by having affairs, or playing Second Life or World of Warcraft, or living in the closet, or being deeply involved in the Internet, or whatever. For me, for years, I chased either love or writing, and they never seemed to live in the same place. So I would live with one and fly to the other.

It started when I moved to Iowa to attend the Writers' Workshop and my girlfriend stayed in New York. For two years we flew to each other once a month. Those visits, a weekend or a week, were like airplane rides themselves: contained, temporary, a pressurized air to them. When I moved back to Brooklyn our land legs failed us and we broke up in three months. We had traveled well. But once we had landed in the same place, it became clear how much each of us had changed in the other's absence.

So when the next opportunity came I was determined not to make the same mistake.

I had received a Stegner Fellowship at Stanford, and I persuaded my reluctant new girlfriend to move from Portland to the Bay Area with me—I was determined for once not to be long-distance. I wanted my life to be intact in one place.

Four months after we had settled in an overpriced North Berkeley bungalow, she was back in Portland house-shopping. To make a long story short, we broke the lease and moved back to Oregon during the break between my winter and spring trimesters, and I started buying up $59 tickets on Southwest.

I could provide astonished co-Stegners and Portlanders alike with abundant rationalizations that involved comparative cost of living, her band obligations, the allure of home-ownership, the unbearable smugness of Berkeley. But deep down I was afraid the long distance would ruin us. I thought, this time I'm going to commute for writing, not love. So while my fellow Stegners drove forty minutes from San Francisco and Oakland, I boarded the predawn light rail to the plane to the shuttle bus to the train to the final bus that cruised down the palm-lined main drive of Stanford and dropped me off in front of Margaret Jacks Hall by noon.

It was crazy, this commute, yet it worked. I couldn't believe how well it worked, and how much I liked it. I surrendered myself to the interlocking schedules of each link. I was blissfully powerless; all I could do and had to do was wait, and the next conductor would show up and take me where I needed to go. Once a week, I knew exactly what was going to happen.

Which was more than I could say for my increasingly uncertain life at home. So when the relationship fell apart at summer's end and I moved out, I did not do the sensible thing and pack up for California. San Francisco was lovely but too much like New York: no space, no quiet, never enough money to live the life you want. I couldn't bear the thought of going from cohabitating in a house to sharing an apartment with strangers for roommates. In Portland I had made friends and I loved the slow pace of things, the dark trees and quiet and lushness. I could live alone and I could take the light-rail to the airport in the morning and be home by midnight. I decided to keep staying and to keep flying.

Mornings would still be dark and cool when I left, carrying nothing but my laptop backpack. I parked my Colt hatchback on a quiet residential block by the Hollywood MAX station and rode the near-empty train to the airport. The plane took off and we rose above the perpetual Portland cloud layer into the rising sun, and when I landed in San Jose the sky would be bright blue and hot, a different light. From piney gloom to beige stucco and red-roof tiles and seasonless sunshine and the palatial Stanford campus where I met my colleagues and we talked about stories. After workshop, I had enough time for dinner and a drink before I retraced my steps back. The last flight to Portland, landing before midnight, just in time to step onto the last train home in the damp night air.

I was an unlikely jetsetter, broke as can be, traveling in sneakers and a dog-chewed backpack. While my fellow fellows TA'ed for Stanford professors and did yoga in the Mission, I, back in Portland, took a job at a scrappy midcentury-modern antique shop for ten bucks an hour. Thursday through Saturday, I swept and dusted and photographed vintage detritus for eBay. Fancy men and women from the West Hills came in and chatted about their Knolls or their paintings or whatever. Sometimes a well-groomed customer would express pleased surprise that I knew what, say, Herman Miller was. Herman Miller. Come on. But to them I was not a writer, I was a shopgirl. And I was. They saw me take out the trash and get my boss coffee. That's what you do for ten bucks an hour. You can sell it but you can't own it.

Is it any wonder I loved those Tuesdays in flight? Flight is, after all, a form of flee too. For one day a week, I led another life that belonged only to me. It was so pure. When I was in the air, no one could ask anything of me: not my boss, not my ex, not my cats, not my friends. I could do nothing but be exactly where I was. Flight gave me purpose: at a time when my sense of direction was confounded, when my inner compass seemed to have lost its true north, those weekly flights put me on my only reliable track toward something. I became a regular. At San Jose, they stopped making me take off my sneakers at security, the guy would just nod me through. I knew where to find the hidden sockets to plug in my laptop. The smell of the Portland airport still triggers in me a deep sense of well-being.

Flight was the most stable thing I knew. Just as speed calms the hyperactive child, transit stilled me.

When the fellowship ended, I missed my flight pattern.

Enough that the next spring I signed on to teach a fabulist-fiction workshop and resumed my weekly trips. But the ticket prices had gone up. The class was in the evening, so I couldn't fly back the same night; instead I slept on friends' couches in the Mission and took the BART to Oakland in the morning. I was barely breaking even. The cost of flight had caught up to me.

I may never again travel so lightly, so freely, so readily. But I have learned—am learning—to sit still. Now I let my restless characters do the running. Flight is easy. Staying is where the real work and the real rewards begin to finally happen.

My Mother's Presence in the Universe

Lucy Corin

A bored friend of mine had driven me to the airport and we talked about boredom. We felt it but remained skeptical about it defining our generation. I said I was keeping an eye out for something to happen in my life that would blow my mind. I said I felt like I'd heard everything before and when would I encounter a new idea? Maybe when someone I love dies, I said, because that had never happened to me. The friend told me about her uncle's funeral when she was eight, looking up at his coffin and seeing only the curved edge of his nose like the distant fin of a shark.

I said, "Did you love him?" and she said, "Not really, but he was definitely dead."

"So the death was like the distant fin of a shark," I said.

We lived in the city, in order to be going someplace. The flight was to visit home, and I felt virtuous because my mother was depressed and needy. It was going be bare—the gentle landscape, always muddy that time of year, with a thin gray sky, and beyond every flat-roofed house along the wavy roads, a human splotch wearing plaid in a field. It was not that big a plane, not that nice a plane, but I didn't know the difference because I didn't fly much. This was a long flight for me at four hours. It started day and landed into the night. I wouldn't even see that landscape until I woke in the dusty bed my mother had tried to make nice for me.

This was also before they filled planes up. My row was somewhere behind the exit rows but not up against the toilets. I had the aisle, no one was in the middle, and there was a woman in the window seat, staring out the window, dirty blond hair down her shoulders, wearing plaid, maybe a little older than me, but not much. Maybe, in retrospect, just looked older. I took out my book. It was still audio-only with occasionally screens up the aisle. I was never a techy-media person anyhow. Later I made a rule in my life where I could buy a trashy magazine only for an airplane, and later I made a rule about TV only on airplanes. I'd find it hard to get off the plane in the middle of a show, some anger about outside forces cutting me off, the force on me of even the basest possible narrative arc, like the getting on and later off an airplane. But I'm not doing the wireless, not even now. I still like to be a little behind the curve and a little judgey about people who keep up and think that means they're caught-up.

I wonder what I could have been reading. I wonder how I went from reading to being in a conversation with her. I think I felt her shaking, looked up, and she was looking right at me, shaking, like *do something about this.*

"Do you fly a lot?" she said. I took it as a compliment.

She said, "I think we're going to die." She had a fleck of something on her lip but it didn't disgust me.

Well, I stepped right up. What on earth did I do? I know I didn't have anything like data of how crashes hardly ever happen, and I'd never heard of "breathing." Did I touch her? Daphne. By the time the cabin doors were closed I knew her name. She clutched either her seat arm or my hand on a seat arm, I don't remember, which shows you how connected I felt, to conflate myself with an inanimate object holding her. What magic words did I spew that got us off the ground? She cried and said very fast through an awful clenched face all the way up: "We're going to die, we're going to die, we're going to die."

But when we leveled off she changed completely. Her face became broad, placid, vibrant. I looked for a remnant of tears and saw none. I felt great about myself. I'd felt like such an outsider growing up with girls who turned into women like her, unlike women like me, who moved to the city with their awesome bored friends. I indulged some reveries about bumping into girls like that when I got home: I spotted their wandering kid at a mall, I fixed their flat on a road, they called me out of the blue and, you know, I was great. When I noticed Daphne again she'd apparently already pushed her flight-attendant button, done some financial exchange right over my lap, and was cheers-ing me with a tiny bottle and then dumping its contents into its plastic cup of ice.

"This is so fucking life affirming, I can't tell you," she said. "I been through some shit. Men shit, money shit, you name it shit. But I am turning a corner. I can feel it. Let me tell you, I was scared, friend. But here we are, and cheers to us. Cheers to us and fucking airplanes." She clucked and chuckled. I knew just what it felt like to be her, elated in suddenly fresh air that is not actually fresh. I told her she was so brave. I ordered a drink, too. I think it was wine. I had a little thing of rosewater to spritz on myself and let her spritz herself with it. "That's nice!" she said, looked at the label, and moved her lips to memorize it.

I took up my reading again. Camus, Hamsun, Dostoyevsky? I mean I like those books but I also know what I liked to prop between my face and strangers. I went deep in there until it must have been some sound linked to the text—a snake in the leaves by the creek outside the house I grew up in where I was going—that made me look over at her again, and when I did she was on another emotional planet. Some amount of little tips of bottles were peeking out of her seatpocket like fingers, and how could I have missed her getting them from the fight attendant? That's the inertia of what you think is going on zooming past what is actually going on. She started talking again: she was on her way home after rehab, she had fucked her life up so much, caused so much pain to the people she loved, she couldn't even tell me the terrible things she'd done, no one should forgive her, a child her friend was keeping for her, stealing from her father, hitting her boyfriend, him hitting back, she'd fucked someone, she was supposed to tell him, to begin to make amends. "I can't face him.

None of them. When I get off this airplane I'm going to a motel, I know just the one. Do you know the one over on Airport Boulevard that has a sign with the arrow through the heart?"

"You could get a good night's sleep," I said. "See him in the morning."

"That's the motel I always wanted to kill myself in."

So that got me scrambling on the inside yet cool, cool on the surface with lots of crisis-intervention ideas to offer her about not being alone, bathtaking, time passing, the pure love of animals, did she have a pet? But everyone hated her and she couldn't face any of them. Then for a moment she could, it was going to be fine, they would see that she had cleaned up, then nope, she could never, never face them, she was going to the motel with the arrow through the heart, it was destiny, she had always known it since she first lay eyes on—what did she say? She said, "first laid eyes on it," and then when she came back around to that part of the circle she said, "first laid eyes on him." I remember that perhaps because I was leaning over the empty middle seat with my hand on her armrest but *her* hands kept moving around, touching the seatpocket and then the control panel on the ceiling, but not doing anything. She took her seatbelt off as if she were going to get up and leave but then put it back on. She moved the windowshade up and then partway down and then up again, and that is just like yanking a stranger's eyelid. "I'll get one more drink, no I won't, I need it, it doesn't matter," around and around and there seemed to have been more drinks and also not more drinks, just as I seemed to have convinced her to call her friend named Lori who seemed the best chance of a person who didn't hate her, "just in case," I said. "You could be wrong, and you don't want to kill yourself and then be wrong." Ok, she'd call Lori. But then, she had always wanted to kill herself in that very motel with the heart with the arrow through it. Then back around to Lori via my incredibly insightful empathetic logic, then around again so that I do not remember how I got off the plane, only an evil battle somewhere behind the exit rows of my mind about whether it was better for her and the rest of the world to just die if she really wanted to, and an image of her in the motel room with the heart, not yet dead, sitting on the edge of the bed looking at something in her hands that I couldn't see, even in my own imagination, and sure as shit not thinking about me or any words I'd said.

I made it through the airport along the walkway toward baggage past murals in tribute to tobacco, and there was my mother to pick me up because this was before homeland security. And if this will say anything about the quality of my mother's presence in the universe, by the time I made it from seeing her among the conveyor belts to giving her whatever greeting we made in those days (I can't picture touching her, but I know we must have touched)—Daphne—and I do not actually remember her name, I just made that up and pretended it was true because I have no memory of what her name was or if we ever exchanged names, names are just placeholders for human beings anyhow— but Daphne disappeared like the fin of a shark into the waters of my mother's presence like a plane going down ironically—but I hope you know how much I mean it.

The visit was okay. My mother and I annoyed each other but also made each other laugh and she was, I don't know, mothery but in a nice way.

Within a few years quite a number of terrible things had happened. Life experiences. The gruesome deaths of some distant relatives, the gruesome deaths of some beloved animals, the gruesome destruction of the lives of people near and dear. The economy collapsed on the radio and throughout the community. On television, there was an entire show dedicated to nostalgia for secretly savvy stewardesses who wore fantastic shoes and strode through the smoke of a thousand sexy cigarettes gliding above a country where stewardesses were stewardesses and assholes turned out to be people with their own demons. On real airplanes people could spend the entire ride comparing loyalty plans and think they'd gotten to know each other. Kill me now if they had, right?

Back on that flight with Daphne, ten minutes before our final descent, we hit some turbulence. She clutched her armrests. "I want to die," she said, and then she said, "We're going to die," and then she said, "I want to die," and then she said, "We're going to die." You can imagine the many tones of voice she used when saying these words. Were there even any other people on the plane at this point? I remember no one. Where I definitely didn't know shit, though, is with regard to my mother, who over the years just went down and down, body as airplane, her brain her very own pilot who eventually tells the control tower how much he loves his wife, and in the final seconds takes his fancy hat in his hands, shuts his eyes, does nothing.

Going to See a Man about a Dog

Alicia Catt

I don't want to tell you that I am a hooker. That story's old news. I don't want to tell you that in my luggage, I've packed twenty condoms and two vibrators, six changes of lingerie, three pairs of fuck-me heels and enough personal lubricant to fill a kiddie pool. I don't want to tell you that I hate this gig, sometimes. I don't want to tell you that sometimes I love it.

What I want to tell you is that it's 2005 and I'm flying alone for the first time, from Minneapolis to Philly, to visit a regular customer. Because I'm twenty-two and occasionally naïve, I think $800 for three days of unlimited access to my body is a pretty good deal. It's not. But when your income depends on the sexual whims of others, you take what you can get when you can get it.

Kent, my Philadelphian client, is a cheap piece of shit. I like him. The first time we met, in Minneapolis, he bought me a single red rose and then, the next morning, showed me how to steal breakfast from the hotel's a-la-carte banquet. He's a touring children's-book author who writes bad poems with worse titles like "Homework Soup" and "Miss McGee's Missing Bees." He's got this wiry grey-brown beard-hair that somehow gets lodged in the nook between my two front teeth whenever we kiss. He's got a small dick. He doesn't really know how to use it.

But he's not a bad man. We talk about literature and philosophy. Bukowski, de Beauvoir. He treats me like a woman, or a girl that could become a woman with a bit of coaxing. When I ask him about his poems he rolls his eyes, says *They're trash and you know it,* and then signs his newest book for me: *Sadie, it was REALLY great meeting you! Best, Kent.*

In the seventy-two hours I'm in Philly—that's $11 an hour, if you're counting—we'll drink martinis at a South Street tapas joint until we're falling over and I'll let him grab my tits in full view of the bartender. He'll do something to piss me off and I'll scrub the toilet with his toothbrush, then feel bad, confess and accept my compensatory spankings. He'll still pay me. He'll even give me a $20 tip before I leave to go home. *Don't spend it all in one place, kiddo.* I will—two trashy magazines and two vodka tonics while waiting to board my return flight.

But right now none of that matters, because I'm just some big-eyed, mouse-haired girl sitting in a Northwest jet on a Minneapolis runway, waiting for takeoff. A girl with soupy, sweat-stained armpits from hauling her scandalous carry-on fifteen blocks to the train to save on airport parking fees. A girl who took her shoes off and paraded, awkward and obedient, through security. A girl sandwiched between two suitcoats that eye her up and down, hungrily or haughtily, before returning to their Palm Pilots.

Please direct your attention to the front of the cabin. I refuse to watch the safety demonstration. I keep my earbuds in and fiddle with my SkyMall instead. Acknowledging the chance of disaster feels like accepting the inevitability of death, and I'm not going to die today. Not with an entire palace of pleasure in my purse, I'm not. What would the coroner think?

The man in the window seat is trying to force small talk already as we taxi. *Philadelphia, eh?* I nod, look down at my trembling hands, say nothing. *You look like you know how to have a good time,* is what I hear. Because my paranoia sometimes overcomes me at times like this, and because I'm a little drunk already, I wonder if he knows. I wonder if everyone knows—the stewardess, the mothers hushing their wrinkled offspring, the motherless teens sitting across the aisle, limbs akimbo. I wonder if they can smell the whore on me like a sickness, the sour scent of latex seeping from my pores. Clogging up the recycled cabin air. Making it so desperately hard to breathe in here.

I white-knuckle my seat cushion on liftoff as though it could, in case of emergency, billow into a soft cotton parachute—cradle me—set me safely on solid ground again.

For Flight Attendants Giving Safety Speeches

Matthew Vollmer

Forgive us, O LORD, for not looking, for averting our eyes, for opening the SkyMall magazine even though we couldn't truly be said to be interested in Roland the Gargoyle Sculptural Rainspout or the Tranquil Sounds Oxygen Bar. Forgive us too for scrolling through our phones and powering up our electronic readers or twisting the plastic doohickeys above our heads to decrease the stale-smelling airflow pouring onto our faces. We are ashamed, LORD, to watch these ladies—and yes, LORD, those Attendants who are women are all ladies, by which we mean strong and selfless arbiters of hospitality—as they do the thing they are, by law, required to do, and the thing that they, in fact, are paid to do, which is to deliver pertinent information concerning what nobody wants to think about, which is what to do and how to proceed if the giant vehicle we all will soon ride into the sky somehow malfunctions, or a Canadian goose flies into a turbine, and pilots are forced to crash land into earth or water. And while we fear dying, LORD, the truth of the matter is that we also fear that we will be caught watching the Attendants during their speeches, that our fellow passengers will notice our forward-looking gaze and cast judgment upon us, because we don't want to give the impression that we are new enough to air travel to not ignore the safety speech. It's not that we don't think the safety speech is important, LORD; we do. And it's not that the safety speech itself doesn't ignite the fuse of our fear, which, in moments like these, can be palpable, as we admit to having faith in the ability of a giant winged capsule to launch us and other strangers to a cruising altitude of 33,000 feet, and despite knowing words like "turbine" and "wingspan," we don't have any idea how this machine works, and why—like cars steering off embankments—more planes simply don't fall out of the sky. We also don't know what our Flight Attendant is thinking, or if she feels awkward, or if feeling awkward is old hat, and thus is not awkward at all. We don't know how many times she had to practice before she memorized the speech in its entirety or, as seems to be the case nowadays, mastered the timing required to synchronize the buckling and pulling-taut of the safety belt while a pre-recorded voice describes its fastening, or the placing over her head of the oxygen mask with the instructions to do so, and though we recognize that there's a sort of off-putting, automated quality to most of these speeches/pantomiming, we definitely notice when the actor—that is, our Attendant—takes the role seriously, by which we mean that she doesn't look bored but pleasantly engaged with this activity or that she never gives up trying to maintain eye contact with the uninitiated few who are actually paying attention, as this imbues her with a kind of authority that, whether we take the time to recognize it or not, allows us to be more comfortable, to settle back in our seats, and subsequently makes us more likely to stow our electronic equipment during take-off and landing, as we would hate to disappoint someone with such an authoritative yet convivial presence. Furthermore, LORD, protect our Attendant, post-safety-speech, for that is when many of us—and we're not proud of this, but it happens—will eyeball her, will note the hip-hugging skirt, the collared shirt open enough to reveal an expanse of neck flesh, and the absence of a ring on her left hand, and embark upon a detailed fantasy in which we might, in some alternate universe, have occasion to meet her later at an airport bar, and saying something like, "Hey, I remember you," and "You were the Attendant on my flight," to which she'd maybe raise an eyebrow while snatching a complimentary pretzel from wax-paper-lined basket, and say something like, "Yep. That's me," and although she's suffered this same rigmarole on many occasions, has been approached by her share of admirers, or those who are merely curious about the life of a Flight Attendant—a life that is, let's be honest, so often and rightly romanticized—she'd say "Sure" when we ask if we might buy her a drink—a vodka tonic, or another glass of Merlot—and if we're lucky (and, as you know, LORD, in our imaginations we always are), we might hear stories about the places our Attendant has visited, how she once listened to a symphony at the Singapore Botanic Garden or tried mulukhiyah in Dubai or shopped for trinkets in Abidjan's Treshville market, and that her favorite place to stay is the Kempinski Hotel in Budapest, one of the cheapest luxury hotels in the world, where she's quite fond of following a full-body massage with a dinner of Black Spaghetti with Fried Seafood and Tomatoes. Of course, it's not all glamor and glitz. There was that one time when the turbulence was so bad over the Atlantic that our Attendant—bless her heart—had to shut her eyes and bite her lip and think about the pale-blue water lit by lantern light at a Tahitian bungalow. And maybe she tells the story of the spilled coffee. Or how, in some countries, when you touch down and pick up passengers, it's totally legit to walk up and down the aisle with a can of air freshener, to reduce the odor of bodies that consume pungent herbs and rarely bathe. Maybe she tells us how she hates it when travelers ask for Diet Coke, because the drink's particular fizz takes three times longer to pour than the average soft drink. Maybe she tells us that she has a son who dropped out of community college and is touring Europe in a hardcore band. Maybe she has a daughter studying Human Nutrition at a State University. Maybe her husband killed himself, or left her, or died of a pulmonary embolism, or still loves her, or never existed. Maybe our Attendant is lonely or fine with being alone, or perfectly happy, or jaded, or vengeful, or taking online courses so she can finish a Bachelor of Arts in Religious Studies. Maybe she imagines, during each and every takeoff, that the Boeing 787 in which she travels, and which is the first line of aircraft to be built with composite materials, will take a sudden nose-dive, and that on this day she and the passengers to whom she attends will be incinerated by a giant ball of flame. Maybe. The truth is, LORD, we don't know. And, in all likelihood, we never will. And probably, we shouldn't. Because we're pretty sure that the last thing our Attendant wants, LORD, and of this we can be quite certain, is to be the subject of our assumptions, or to come alive, as it were, in our imaginations. So please, LORD, let us avert our gaze. Let us not order Diet Coke. And, as we depart, let us thank her for her service, and wish her a heartfelt and sincere goodbye.

In Between Days

Julian Hanna

Future wife and I were waiting at SFO to catch a post-Christmas flight back to Edinburgh, Scotland, where we lived at the time. It was the second leg of a lengthy tour to meet both our families: first my mother in Victoria, BC, and then her oldest sister, standing in for the mom she had recently divorced after one-too-many family blowouts, in Gilroy, California. The holidays had passed without serious incident and we were cleared for matrimony the following September.

Cleared for marriage, but not for takeoff. The departures board was showing a snow delay at Heathrow. Outright cancellation followed a few hours later. We greeted this news with an emotional sequence that went: indignation, resignation, relief. Relief because we didn't have to wait anymore, and we were in no hurry to exchange California for dull, freezing Scotland. We had booked with a good airline, for once, and they offered us a hotel. This seemed like a grand luxury after two weeks of improvised bedding in family guest rooms. We could even stay two nights if we wanted.

We sauntered off a few paces to discuss the matter, and then returned to announce that we would take two nights. There was another, unannounced part of the plan: that we would not contact friends or, especially, local relatives. Our obligations had been fulfilled: this leg of our trip would be a pre-wedding honeymoon. I called to cancel my slot at an academic conference in Glasgow, and she called her boss to register her absence. Then we boarded the little bus and celebrated our arrival at the Airport Marriott with umbrella cocktails on the patio of the hotel bar. It rained, but we decided that was what the little umbrellas were for.

The weird thing about airport hotels is that they are full of airport staff. I don't know if this is always the case, but during our stay the bar, restaurant, lobby, and elevators were fully stocked with men and women in uniform. Their colors and wing markings seemed to indicate rank and corporate allegiance. They swapped jabs at each others' companies under the guise of false smiles. The other guests were uniformed to such an extent that I remember feeling distinctly uncomfortable in civilian clothes. Each passing visage, the men and the women alike, bore the dull sheen of heavy makeup under a sturdy roof of hairsprayed bouffant. There was a lot of manmade fabric, too, from the stain-resistant Olefin carpets to the polyamide microfiber crew suits. In this context, I could see the wisdom of the smoking ban that had been passed recently in California.

On our first day we did everything our logical minds told us to: we rode the BART into San Francisco, walked around the city, drank a lot of coffee, ate at a good Vietnamese place, and saw all the sights. Though neither of us could say why, this bonus day of tourism tacked on to the end of our trip was exhausting and slightly underwhelming. We returned to the anonymity of the Marriott at dusk and ate a meal of oily vegetarian-option pasta in the Applebee's next door.

The kitsch value of the airport holiday was wearing thin. We sniped at each other over dinner. We argued about whose family had been more exhausting to deal with, and whose work was suffering more by our prolonged absence. Then we made up, and when we got back to our ticky-tacky room we tried to breathe some animal warmth into it with exaggerated gestures of lovemaking. After forty minutes of breathy flight attendants and handsome pilots in steamy stopover scenarios, we slept.

The next day we broke out of the familiar feeling of obligation that plagues most holidays. We swapped our guilt and our slavish obedience to clock time for spontaneity and embraced the moment. Our flight was at five o'clock that evening. We got to the airport right after breakfast and stowed our bags and still had seven hours to kill.

We decided to check out the neighborhood. We left through the automatic doors and started down the highway, taking a smaller road at the first exit. Being on foot in the land of cars and shuttles was awkward, dangerous, and possibly even illegal, but we kept walking. We walked past razor-wire fences, studied patterns of debris in the ditches, and stood aside holding hands as anonymous traffic roared past. There were no bicycles, no sidewalks, no public parks, no residential housing of any kind. There were warehouses and self-storage buildings, a few chain restaurants, and lots of empty space.

But this no man's land was far from barren. The warm winter sun, hidden behind clouds for much of our visit, now set us free: we stripped to our t-shirts and picked wild flowers by the roadside, fashioning daisy chains and boutonnières. After the bleak midwinter of Scotland this seemed an enchanted, if slightly post-apocalyptic, tropical paradise. When we reached the perimeter of the runway area we found that the planes shared the land with a bird sanctuary, and we stood at the fence watching cormorants, loons, and herons, hunting and diving, pursuing mates, fighting with rivals, all amid the constant disruption of takeoffs and landings. We kissed for a long time at the fence and then started our walk back to the terminal, knowing we had passed a more important test than the banter with relatives and all the hurdles of the previous week. We knew that we approved of each other.

Free Beer

Thomas Gibbs

I was flying back from my mother-in-law's funeral. My wife had stayed behind. Finishing a Heineken and ready to order another, I noticed the man in front of me jerk his right arm out into the aisle. His head flew back into the seat.

I am not a neurologist, but I know full-blown seizures. All I wanted was another beer. Or two. This was a perfect time for a beer. I wanted one right then. Waiting would not work. I couldn't believe this passenger was sick in the middle of a flight.

I did what I could: I got up and made sure the man was breathing. The lights were off, it was dark, and my reading light provided the only illumination. He was in the first row—I was in the second. No flight attendants were in the front of the plane. I lifted the front overhead baggage door to look for an oxygen tank, and then I saw the man have a second seizure.

I glanced toward the back of the plane; the silhouettes of three airline attendants approached. The man was finally conscious enough to answer questions. "Do you have a seizure disorder?" I asked.

"No," he replied, "but I am three weeks out of a triple cardiac bypass. They misdiagnosed me at first."

"What other medical problems do you have? High blood pressure? Diabetes?"

"Both" he said, "and I have been sick with nausea and vomiting for two days. I can't keep anything down."

What does he think he's doing on a plane, I thought to myself. I asked if he had any of his medications with him. He told me he had a nitroglycerin but had never taken it.

"This would be a good time," I said. He opened the nitro bottle and spilled the pills on his lap. I reached to help him, but he found one and put it in his mouth. I passed orange juice for him to drink in case his sugar was low. He swallowed the pill.

"This is a medical emergency," I told the first flight attendant. "We need the O_2 tank now." He fumbled with it as he pulled it down and decided which way to turn the gauge. I pulled the yellow mask over the man's nose and mouth and made sure there was a good flow of oxygen. The second attendant handed me a blood-pressure cuff. I checked the patient's heart rate. His blood pressure was low but I already knew that from his weak, thready pulse. He was soaked in sweat, his color ashen.

"How far are we from landing and getting this man help?" I asked the flight attendant.

"We're thirty minutes out of Orlando," she said. I knew this was the closest city with good medical care, so I asked if there was any way we could get there faster. The attendant headed toward into the cockpit. The second attendant was on the phone with the paramedics preparing them for the patient. I called out his vital signs and she repeated them to the people on the ground.

I also knew I couldn't count on any more beer. "Shit," I cursed under my breath.

The man's wife was sitting across the aisle from him. She had not identified herself at first and did not get up or help. I wondered whether she was frightened or just angry at him for getting on the plane in his condition. I asked her to write down each medication he was taking and every medical condition from which he suffered. I planned to give it to the paramedics when we landed. She asked what had happened. She hadn't noticed anything. "He had a seizure," I said. I did not mention that I could be wrong and he might have had a stroke.

The attendant returned from the cockpit and said that if I called this episode a "medical emergency" air-traffic control could hold off other planes and we would land without delay. I was shocked to think that they couldn't see for themselves what was happening. "Yes, this is an emergency," I said. *Anything in those pretty heads?* I thought.

I laid the man down across the seats. His feet extended out across the aisle. The oxygen and change in position seemed to help; his color improved. I buckled a seatbelt around him. I could feel the plane pick up speed. I braced my back foot to keep my balance.

We landed fast and turned the corner toward the gate. The plane didn't tilt up on one wheel and the wing did not hit the ground, but it seemed to be going too fast. The ambulance was at the gate; its emergency lights flashing. The paramedics came up the steps and I presented my findings to them. I handed them the list of the man's medications and his medical problems. The man lived as long as I was taking care of him; I don't know what happened once he was placed in the ambulance.

Relieved of my patient all I could think was, *Goddamn it, those beers were free with my upgrade.* I looked down at the free-drink coupon on my empty seat.

Then I was faced with all the administrative duties that doctors hate: providing medical license numbers, my address, and DEA certificate. It's the reason some of us don't stand up when asked if there is a doctor on board; there's too much risk and liability. This is the fourth time I have assisted a passenger in the middle of a flight. Each time I respond I swear it will be the last.

I looked at the wife as she headed down the steps behind the stretcher and said, "Tell your husband he has a gynecologist now." She didn't see the humor.

My Czechoslovakian Plastic Surgeon

Tarn Wilson

He sat in the window seat, immersed in a magazine. I registered little about him other than he'd crossed his legs, he wore cuffed business slacks, and his thick hair was graying at the temples.

A second magazine, *Time*, lay on the empty seat between us. I don't remember its cover, but I understood the moment I saw it that I was starved for news of the world. I was eighteen, on my way home to Colorado for winter break after my first semester of college, a small liberal-arts school in the Midwest circled by cornfields. I'd become deliciously immersed in the eighteenth-century Romantic poets, but—in those years before the Internet or TVs in every dorm room—I'd lost touch with the present.

So I turned to the gentleman and asked if I could borrow his extra magazine. I smiled. He smiled. Still, I didn't really notice him—I was so attracted to that bright-red cover.

I'd already disappeared into the first article, when he interrupted.

I didn't want to talk. I was exhausted from my first finals. But I didn't want to be unkind.

I put the magazine on my lap and turned to the man. He was, he told me, from Czechoslovakia. A plastic surgeon. On his way to an international conference in Vail. Did I want to see his nose jobs?

I did. I really did. My family collected amusing anecdotes, and his question was fabulously peculiar. And who doesn't like before-and-after pictures? He took out an enormous three-ringed binder with page after page of photographs in plastic sleeves. Noses snipped, shortened, narrowed, remolded like· putty. Unsmiling people with pale, greenish faces. Front shots. Profiles. He ordered another little bottle of alcohol. Did I want one, too?

No. No, thank you.

My mind wandered toward the ethics of plastic surgery, how sad that already-lovely women, with just the slightest bump on the top or ball of their noses, were carving themselves up, destroying that very feature that gave them character. But then there were those very large or odd noses and the question became more complex.

But he'd moved on to other topics. In Czechoslovakia, he had a wife. He had two children, a son and a daughter, whom he loved very much. "My daughter," he said, "she's just about your age." I nodded and smiled.

Then, before I realized what he'd done, he was in the seat next to me. I could smell the tang of his drink on his breath, his flowery aftershave. He pressed his shoulder into mine. I leaned as far as I could into the aisle. I glanced down the walkway to see if a flight attendant might pass anytime soon and help extricate me. One walked by and carefully edged her way around my body. Again, he crossed his legs and with his dangling foot began to caress my calf.

"You come with me," he said in his heavy Czech accent. "I have a condo in Vail. You stay with me in my condo."

My mind scrambled. He had a daughter my age. He had a wife. He had a bag full of noses! But I'd not yet learned how to be rude.

I froze, then blurted: "I don't think my mother would like that." Perfect. I wasn't rejecting him personally. At the same time, I was subtly reminding him of our ages and families.

Too subtly. He leaned more heavily into me and answered, "You tell your mother I'm a dok-tor. She won't mind."

Game over. He had crossed some line into ridiculousness. I laughed. I don't remember what happened next, only that I was free of him and had tucked away a story to share.

The other day, I was exercising in the gym and caught a man glancing at me. He ran his fingers through his hair and I could see an elaborate tattoo ringing his left bicep. He moved to the machine next to me. In my peripheral vision I could see him trying to catch my eye, find the opening line. I was curious about him—his scruffy hair and weary face—and what was that tattoo?

But in the many years since that airplane ride, I've learned—most of the time, anyway—not to let curiosity or pathological politeness override my intuition. I've mastered the art of The Ignore. I looked ahead as if I hadn't seen my tattooed man, counted my way through my repetitions, moved to the next machine.

Yet, even as I'm convinced The Ignore is the safer route, I also know that in the trade, I've sacrificed something: satchels full of noses and a story to tell.

Until We Land

Susan Hodara

For the last four hours of our flight from Nice to New York, the man's body lay across the middle seats of the row behind us. The flight attendants had draped red airline blankets along the tops of the seatbacks and tented them over him. They'd wrapped his calves and feet, which extended into the aisle so that passengers had to step over them on their way to and from the restrooms. The man's wife hunkered in the window seat across from him, staring blindly ahead.

It was the end of our week-long trip to Provence, where my husband, Paul, and I had attended a wedding, then driven the serpentine roads of the Alpes-de-Haute-Provence. A couple of hours after takeoff, I looked up from my book to find Paul standing beside our seats talking to a flight attendant. He was offering to help her open the bathroom door nearby, suggesting she use the metal end of a loose seatbelt for better leverage on the emergency release. It was like him to get involved when he spotted something amiss.

"What's going on?" I asked.

He turned toward me and spoke in a lowered voice. "Someone collapsed in there," he said.

"How do you know?"

"His wife got worried when he didn't come back to his seat. Now he's on the floor, and they can't open the door."

I loosened my seatbelt and twisted around so I could see. The wife, on the opposite side of the plane, was pacing up and down the aisle. She looked to be around seventy, a petite woman with straight auburn hair cut short. She wore khaki pants and a matching shirt. Her face was flushed, her mouth set tight.

I shifted up onto my knees. They will manage to open the

door, I thought. They will revive the man, help him up, bring him back to his wife. He will sit with her until we land.

But the door was still jammed. While Paul edged closer to the bathroom, I remained seated. I told myself there was nothing I could do, but I know now that I was also stung by the horror of what might be.

Finally, the door was forced open. By this point, the passengers in the nearest row had been moved, and the pilot had joined the group. He and a male attendant unfolded the man from the stall, one grabbing under his arms, the other taking his feet. There wasn't enough room and the body sagged until someone stepped in to support it. When they lay the man along the empty seats, his shirt was unbuttoned. I could not see his face, but I saw his belly flecked with white hair, a scar from what might have been an appendectomy dipping below his belted pants. His left arm had been shoved by the seatback across his body; his hand rested palm down on his ribs, watch on his wrist, gold wedding ring on his finger.

There was a flurry of activity around him. Much of what was taking place was blocked from my view, but I could see the up-and-down of a doctor who was on board pressing over and over on the man's chest. The wife came back down the aisle. "Il est morte, il est morte," she said, until an attendant urged her back to her seat.

It was at least fifteen minutes that the man had been in the bathroom, and another half hour before there was some kind of consensus that the intervention should stop. The doctor was sweating. One of the attendants was crying.

I looked for the wife, who had returned to her husband. She stood as if frozen, and I mirrored her, immobilized in my seat. I thought of Paul, with his high blood pressure, sitting endlessly at the computer, then pushed the image from my mind.

Even though, for the rest of the flight, the body's presence filled the plane, and the heavy shadows of loss and fragility pressed down around us, I couldn't find my emotions. From time to time, I peered back at the man, so I could feel once more the jolt of his death. But what really compelled me was his wife—his widow, I said to myself.

I wanted to study her, watch her for clues. She'd wrapped herself in an airline blanket. I saw her take out her cell phone, then put it back in her purse. It wasn't until we landed, and she took out the phone again, that I saw her tears.

But for all those hours in the air, whenever I turned to look at to her—and I did it often, I couldn't stop myself—her eyes were on mine, as if she had gotten there first to deflect me, and I had to look away.

Seat Assignment

Nina Katchadourian

Clock (Gold), 2014

While in the lavatory on a domestic flight in March 2010, I spontaneously put a tissue-paper toilet-seat cover over my head and took a picture in the mirror using my cell phone. The image evoked fifteenth-century Flemish portraiture. I decided to add more images made in this mode and planned to take advantage of a long-haul flight from San Francisco to Auckland, guessing that there were likely to be long periods of time when no one was using the lavatory on the fourteen-hour flight. I made several forays to the bathroom from my aisle seat, and by the time we landed I had a large group of new photographs entitled *Lavatory Self-Portraits in the Flemish Style*. This series is now part of a larger series called *Seat Assignment*, which is an ongoing art project made on airplanes, using only my cell phone and the materials I find around me.

Engine Failure, 2012

The works fall into three of the most timeless art-historical genres: still life, portrait, landscape. The plane's interior is a landscape unto itself, one that exists between two other landscapes: the one the traveler has just left, and the one the traveler is returning to. The traveler might be dreaming of either, but usually, the traveler is not trying to fully inhabit either the landscape of the plane or the psychological space of the present moment. More often than not, a traveler tries to escape from the physical and psychological confines of the airplane and exist somewhere else for the duration of the flight. *Seat Assignment* requires a complete investment in the present moment, the materials at hand, and faith and attentiveness to both.

Pretzel Meteor, 2012

I often make art motivated by the mundane, but *Seat Assignment* has become a vehicle for me to put many of my deeply-held premises to the test. Is there always more than meets the eye? Is there really something to make out of nothing? Is it truly a matter of paying attention, of staying alert and optimistic about the potential that something interesting could evolve when challenged by boredom? Furthermore, what are the limits of my ability to think on my feet (or from my seat)? When will my creativity hit a wall, either from physical and mental fatigue, or simply because I can't care anymore at that moment? How far will my own sense of decorum allow me to go in a public situation?

Lavatory Self-Portrait in the Flemish Style #2, 2011

Images courtesy of the artist and Catharine Clark Gallery.

There and Back

Stewart Sinclair

I wasn't on one of the ostentatious Dreamliners for which Etihad Airlines had poured a small fortune into advertising, going so far as to hire Nicole Kidman as a spokesperson. Although the flight attendants were in fact wearing the Parisian-designed attire that constituted a sort of Saddam Hussein meets Prada look, with a svelte cut, maroon coloring, scarves and little hats reminiscent of the military style that Iraq's former dictator fashioned into an icon for the despotic. This was the Economy version of the Etihad experience—the regular person's treatment for a trip to the country that controls a tenth of the world's oil production, the United Arab Emirates. But it was my first flight to another country, and even in Coach, I found a way to lose myself.

My flight to Abu Dhabi was only half-full. No one else was sitting in my row. I had reserved the window, but it was nice to know that I could have any seat that I wanted, or I could fold up the armrests and lay across all three seats, close my eyes and maybe even dream of the accouterments of Dreamliners.

Sleep wasn't on my mind. I didn't really see a reason, because my favorite part of any plane is that little oblong window that gives you a porthole-sized view of the world for the price of a kink in the neck. I love pressing my forehead against the window and feeling even just the crisp suggestion of the extreme cold air that we're flying through. I like looking at the little dot that forms on the bottom of the window with spider-webbed frostbite emanating from around it. On most flights I indulge in these pleasures with a tinge of guilt, because I feel like I'm obstructing the view of the poor sap whose bad luck landed him in a middle seat. So I tend to lean back on arrival and departure so that they can watch the world whiz by for a brief moment, and then I lean in, and I stay there.

For fourteen hours on-board an aircraft that had been reassigned from the old Delta line-up, I had the solace of open space. I travelled eastward reading *East of Eden*, pausing between chapters to look out the window and watch the rapid succession of the phases of the day, as the sun rose and fell in the sky at twice its normal pace. My only regret was that the dimly lit cockpit and the blinking red light at the end of the wing obfuscated the starry sky, and I was on the wrong side of the plane to see the moon.

I lost count of the snacks and meals that the flight attendants brought me. I assume that they had fully stocked the plane despite its sparse passenger-load. So whenever they passed by, I accepted what they offered—a Coke here, a bag of cookies there, a dinner with a vaguely Middle-Eastern theme. I drank wine in turbulent weather, losing half the cup to a rough patch. The red drops stained the fuselage by my knees, but they gave me another glass.

When I was young I said that I would never leave my hometown. Planes frightened me. Before my first flight my mother slipped me half a Valium to keep me calm. It was just after 9/11, and suddenly every passenger on every plane was suspect. I wouldn't go near our mailbox either (because, you know…anthrax). I don't know how that boy who refused to sleep over at other kids' homes suddenly found himself onboard a flight to the Middle East for a conference on lung disease. Some confluence of chance, luck and tenacity that evolved out of circumstances beyond his control, I suppose. But there I was, and at some time in the night our plane crossed the Atlantic and a yellow haze emanated from 32,000 feet below us. The radial spokes and white-hot centers of European cities; the coast of Spain and the hamlets dotting the hills of France; the lights tracing the banks of the Nile River; the Mediterranean port cities.

In less than a day, I watched the sun set over the Atlantic and watched it rise red and orange over the desert of the Arabian

Peninsula. The sand dunes stretched on in idyllic waves, here and there splotched with crop circles.

As we began our descent I finished reading the final lines of Steinbeck's book, and contemplated the meaning of the word *timshel* as I watched, for the first time, the skyline of another country's capital come into view, goliaths jutting out of the T-shaped peninsula, whose wavy shore is awash in an aqua-marine tint. We descended over marshes unlike any I had ever seen, as well as a giant amorphic structure called Ferrari World, the theme park that boasts the fastest rollercoaster on earth. The plane came to rest on a runway in between the old and neglected Abu Dhabi airport and the skeleton of what will become the new airport, which, as I would come to learn about everything in Abu Dhabi, was a testament to the wealth of a nation, covered with shimmering glass and filled with industrial air-conditioning, inviting tourists upon arrival while revealing nothing of the country's soul.

There ought to be some larger narrative about what transpired while I was in Abu Dhabi. I'm sure that you want to know about the gold malls, or what it's like to hear the call to prayer on a cool evening while standing at the Sheikh Zayed Mosque. You might be interested to know about a man who worked at the mosque named Muhammad, from Sri Lanka, who never stopped smiling, even after I asked him if he would ever go home, even as he simply said, *No.* I would love to tell you about a late night around a pool table in the lobby, when one of the hotel employees named Godspower laughed with us as I tried to teach a colleague how to shoot a pool cue. But the nature of business travel, and of a destination designed for these events, is that all of these experiences are incidental, fleeting moments lost amidst a tide of side-meetings, dinner parties, keynote speakers, and phone calls on official business. As one of my coworkers put it, "I've seen the world through the lens of hotels and convention centers."

A week after arriving, after all of the conferences and dinners and hotel drinks and mosque visits, I was back at the airport. I went through customs, took my seat, and looked out the window, back at the skeletal bones of Abu Dhabi's new airport. That unfinished airport was as close as I would get to seeing what lies under the surface of a place like this.

The whole flight home transpired in a perpetual midday, so the flight attendants asked us to close the covers of the windows. I followed the arc of our flight on the screen in front of me. Abu Dhabi was no longer a place. It was just somewhere that I had been; just a few pixels on the map, eventually disappearing off the edge of the screen as we approached the United States, as if my whole time in Abu Dhabi was as transient as the flight there and back.

Pan Am FA 74113

Jeani Elbaum

After flight-attendant training was complete, the letters clarifying our individual weight requirements were handed out to each one of us. My letter looked like this:

Note to: JEANNETTE ELBAUM
Employee Number: 74113
Class Number: Class 5
On February 23, 1989, your height was recorded at 5′4″ and your frame size was determined to be SMALL. Your weight on that date was recorded at 113.

In accordance with Pan Am's established weight standards, your maximum allowable weight has been set at 123.

In accordance with Pan Am Medical and Flight Service department standards, the maximum allowable weight, as noted above, must not be exceeded during your employment as a Flight Attendant.

I worked a job that at one time was coveted by many. I was a flight attendant for Pan American World Airways, an airline that represents the glamour of the golden age of passenger travel. While working for Pan Am I was based at the Worldport at John F. Kennedy International Airport in New York. Many perceived the job to be glamorous, and at times it was, but often any glamour was overshadowed by the mundane, leaving me feeling intellectually and emotionally conflicted.

My flight-attendant work usually entailed waiting, prepping, assisting, and servicing. It was filled with passengers, the Federal Aviation Administration, and Pan Am regulations, all with their own set of needs and demands.

On international and domestic flights 90 percent of in-air time was spent serving food and beverages to passengers and addressing their other needs. During the five weeks of training in Miami at Pan Am's training academy, flight attendants were provided with a training manual. The number of pages it took to outline the First Class service on a Boeing 747 was 105. Surely this added to the glamour of the Pan Am passenger experience. Their First Class service from beginning to end consisted of six linen-lined serving carts. It began with basic flight amenities such as headphones, dinner menus, newspapers and magazines followed by hors d'oeuvres and caviar; salad, bread and wine; roast beef carved to order along with sides; fruit, cheese and wine; and dessert, coffee and liqueurs. Although Business and Economy Class options were not as extensive, multiple meal and beverage services were offered with a variety of choices for food and drink. In addition, pillows, blankets, magazines and newspapers were the norm on all trans-continental and international flights in all classes of service. Pan Am trained their in-flight service crews to anticipate passenger's needs, not to wait for a request.

In addition to passenger wants and needs, safety was a top priority. In 1903 the United States Congress acknowledged a new industry—air transportation—thereby creating the first federal regulatory control system, which in 1967 would morph into the Federal Aviation Administration (FAA). The FAA is responsible for aviation safety and as a flight attendant you are well aware of the impact an inspector from the agency can have on your flight and your pocketbook should you choose not to enforce one or more of the Federal Air Regulations (FARs). During the late 1980s a flight attendant could be fined as much as $1000 if a safety regulation was not enforced. Along with helping passengers stay in compliance with the FAR's we were required to keep certain items on our person, such as a flashlight, and other items very close to our jump seat, like our flight-service handbook.

Following the FARs was of utmost importance; however, during this phase of air travel, flight attendants bounced around in turbulence while checking to make sure passengers were safely in their seats with fastened seatbelts. Today in-flight service crews keep themselves safe by taking their seats in these situations.

Safety and service were at the top of the list on a flight attendant's duties and it was expected these tasks would be accomplished with grace and beauty. Thus we pushed 200lb bar carts up inclined aisles, wore uniforms made of polyester-wool blend in order to look professional and feminine, yet at the same time withstand spills, sweat and bloating. We accepted required beauty routines involving strict-regulation hairstyles with our hair never allowed to touch our shoulders. Make-up had to be comprised of colors such as blues, pinks and purples to erase the red and puffiness from tired eyes. On our lips and nails we wore bright pinks and reds to add glamour and even more color. Two brands that seemed to have just the right lipstick colors for Pan Am requirements were Revlon and Estée Lauder. It was Estée Lauder who sent their make-up artists to provide makeovers for us on the fourth day of training. From that point forward our make-up, nails and hair were to meet Pan Am's regulation standards.

Since airlines must have a certain number of flight attendants on each flight we had entire months when we were on call a number of days each week. On several occasions I had to get up at 4 a.m. to put on my make-up, groom my hair and then dress in full uniform for what was referred to as a ninety-minute call period—meaning that on this type of reserve I could be called and asked to be at JFK or LaGuardia in ninety minutes to fill in for a no-show flight attendant. I would sit around for hours ready to go, just in case.

However stressful the non-glamour moments were, along the way magic and exoticism would creep in and create the willingness for what was asked of me. I rarely worked more than three days a week and many times my workday ended in Mexico, San Francisco, Paris, Madrid, Frankfurt, London, or Rome. Pan Am no longer exists, but once had the second most recognizable logo in the world. At least that is what they told us our third day in training. I believed it then and still do today.

Pan American World Airways ceased operations in December 1991.

Class Matters

Neal Pollack

I'm betraying my age by revealing this, but I've always loved the *Saturday Night Live* film from the early '80s where Eddie Murphy goes undercover as a white person. He discovers that being white confers even more advantages than he'd thought. A newsstand employee gives him a free paper because no one else is around. When the only other black guy gets off a public bus, suddenly the route becomes a rolling cocktail party. A bank manager hands Murphy $50,000 in cash and tells him he doesn't have to pay it back. "Slowly," Murphy says, "I began to realize that when white people are alone, they give things to each other for free."

That's how I felt when I started flying Business Class.

My entire adult life, I'd flown Economy. Flying, to me, meant long lines, uncomfortable seats, indifferent service, erratic in-flight entertainment, and $6 bags of stale chips. If I wanted to change my reservations, with the exception of a couple of budget airlines, it cost me hundreds of dollars. I always traveled light, but when the carriers began to charge for bag fees, I started traveling with almost nothing. Flying was no more glamorous than the train trip to the airport. As far as I was concerned, there was no other way.

Then, thanks to an astonishing stroke of fortune, I got an assignment to go drive a Bentley convertible. In Croatia. That in itself was miraculous to me, as I never thought I'd visit Croatia in my life, much less drive a Bentley. But even more amazing was that they were flying me to Europe, via Delta, on International Business Class. Two months previous, I'd been forced to move from my home in Los Angeles to a not-as-nice home in Austin. I was living off my security deposit from the old house and found myself saddled with a considerable amount of credit-card debt, a lot of it from old Economy Class airplane tickets that I hadn't paid off yet. I was trapped forever in the 99 percent and had about as much of a chance of flying International Business Class as I did of skiing in the Olympics. Yet when my wife dropped me at the airport, a new world of travel opened. It was as though I'd woken up in the morning and suddenly had a complimentary personal butler.

When you fly Business Class, if you want to check your bag, that's fine, they won't charge you. If you're late for your flight, don't worry about it, because there's a "Premium" line that moves at ten times the speed of the regular one. If you have to interact with an airline employee, they say, "Thank you for your business, sir." All that happened within ten minutes of getting to the airport. I wanted to say, "I'm a fraud! Look at my scraggly beard and my Old Navy button-down! There are holes in my socks!" But they didn't care. I held the golden ticket. The curtain had been pulled back, and they'd let me through.

On the plane, it was even better. The seats reclined into beds. There were menus, and complimentary French wines. You got blankets and earplugs and eye masks, and unlimited choices of movies, some of which were still in the theaters, to watch. The food wasn't great, but it wasn't bad, and there were five courses of it, including a cheese course. They brought you drinks before takeoff, hot nuts soon after, and hot towels at regular intervals. For several hours, I was someone else, or at least an alternate-universe version of myself. Oh, sweet mysteries of life, at last I'd found them!

Since then, I've been flown to Europe on Delta six other times, all of them International Business Class. After the second, I reached Silver Medallion status. That's because when you fly in the front of the plane, they give you *double miles,* and you don't even have to ask for them. Two trips after that, I had my Gold Medallion, and last month, I got my Platinum status. Suddenly, I was getting automatic upgrades on all my domestic flights, and had a private line I could call if I needed to change my reservations or if I just wanted to chat with a friendly voice. This, I began to realize, is what it's like to be, not necessarily white, but definitely rich. People just give things to each other for free.

The benefits to flying in First are infinite. Ground delays mean nothing if your chair reclines into a bed and you get unlimited snacks. But there are some detriments as well. In general, the people in Economy are friendlier. I've met some nice folks up front, but I've also sat next to more than one millionaire next-door who's going to the continent to do some sort of "business," but still thinks it's OK to wear shorts and flip-flops. You're on a work trip to Paris, buddy, I find myself thinking. Put on some decent shoes. Also, that bowling ball under your golf shirt isn't getting any smaller. Maybe you should forgo the airplane beef just this once.

Another big difference: Unless you're on your way to Vegas, people in Economy are generally pretty sober, which is more than I can say for First Class, which is an alcoholic's wet dream. On the way to Spain, I sat next to a guy who drank *eight* vodka tonics and three glasses of wine before he finally threw back his head and began snoring like a cartoon dog. Another time, on a domestic upgrade, I bivouacked by someone who had three Bloody Marys before our 9 a.m. takeoff. I do occasionally take some wine with my dinner over the Atlantic, and I have a hard time saying "no" to the question "Would you like some port?" but I'm under the general impression that drinking while flying is extremely bad for your health. Just because you're an International Business traveler doesn't mean you're immune from severe heart disease.

I'll never give up my Platinum status willingly. Please don't take it away from me, seriously, or I will die. But I'm an impostor. Even though I fly high-end a lot now, I'm still very middle-class, and not upper-middle, either. I can see that there's something resolutely offensive about the extreme class-divide that exists on airplanes. If the people in Coach knew what it was really like up there, especially on international flights, they'd come at us with pitchforks.

The last couple of months, all my flights have been domestic, and I've been flying Southwest. My bags are still free to check, at least the first two, but so it is for the rest of the hoi polloi. I wait in line, jockey for seats, and generally fly without frills, though with seemingly endless bags of peanuts. There are a lot more little old ladies in the cabins, a lot more black people, a lot more college students, and a decent share of business travelers as well. You never know who your seat partner is going to be, which I think is better. In First Class, you almost always know what you're going to get, within one or two standard deviations. Flying Southwest feels more democratic, more American, fairer somehow, more honest.

That said, it'd be nice if they'd offer me a glass of port once in a while.

What is a Winglet?

Christiana Z. Peppard

A suspicion shared by frequent travelers is that New York-La
Guardia may be the unwashed armpit of US airports. This notion
applies especially to Concourse B, where passengers wait to be
raptured to their destinations by AirTran, Southwest, Spirit,
Frontier, and JetBlue. Among its other underwhelming features,
the ceiling in Concourse B has been known to leak, such that blue
mop buckets and gray trash cans appear in uncanny places (the
middle of the walkway, for example) to catch drips. It goes
without saying that you rarely find celebrities in Concourse B:
they stay away or very sensibly fly out of a different, newly
remodeled, concourse. The airport mostly traffics in distances
less than 1500 miles, except for Denver (1785 miles) and
(strangely?) Saturdays.

In my experience, Concourse B at LGA can be compared to an
overcrowded European hostel, the Kathmandu airport in 1999,
or Rockefeller Plaza on a Saturday between Thanksgiving and
Christmas. We proletariat passengers cluster in overcrowded
seating areas, pretending patience, vying for outlets, and
queuing for toilets as we tote more-than-your-allotment "purse
or briefcase" bags piled precariously atop not-quite-overhead-
container-sized suitcases. It is not a place for anyone with fear of
crowds, grime, lines, carpet stains, small children, or coddled lap
dogs—the last of which, according to my observations on the
Tuesday before Christmas 2014, exceeded the number of small
children by a factor of two to one.

It was December 23, and we were going to Denver, where our
daughter had for five days been happily playing with grandparents, aunts, uncles, and cousins in that sun-drenched locale—
while we, the laboring parents, commuted in freezing ice storms

to administer and grade our college students' final exams. We were ready for a change of scenery. I was ready for a change of mood. It seemed that approximately half of the airport's annual traffic of twenty-five-million people, along with my spouse and I, were crammed into Concourse B in anticipation of leaving NYC for the Christmas holiday. Thus my griping about LGA was probably at an all-time high—even as I knew, of course, that we were among the petty bourgeoisie who could afford to describe ourselves as air-travel proletariat and lament the aesthetic pains of our voluntary travels.

After all, we had chosen to fly out of LGA because of its unrivalled proximity to the city and those flights to Denver. And as long as you can tolerate the sight, sound, and scent of your fellow human beings—while sashaying around the most egregious leaks in the ceiling—on a normal day at Concourse B you're likely to get where you're going without incident, usually at the same time as your luggage. It's gritty but reliable. In this sense, the airport might even be emblematic of the lives of so many not-so-rich New Yorkers: determined yet fraying at the edges, we stay for the urban convenience, professional productivity, and because we have just enough to keep aloft. Sure, our margins are tight. We gripe. But we rely on both the city and the airport and are willing to put up with a bit of the unexpected because that's what you do in a city of eight-million people: Crammed together, you do your best to give each other space.

*

Concourse B is so crowded that clambering into a narrow, metal-and-fiberglass row of airplane seats can actually be relaxing. My husband and I settled quickly into seats 6A and B, in front of the wing, as the flight attendants cracked cheery, corny jokes.

Row 6 is nice because the aerodynamic cut of the wing behind you frames one line of sight, but you can also perceive what's ahead and below without the full-noise drone of the engine or the visual obstruction of the wing. Our aircraft, like many contemporary models, had what are known as "winglets," a design feature that increases the efficiency of flight by reducing drag on the tip of the wing as well as helping to maintain airfoil lift—a desirable thing from an aerodynamic perspective. It's also useful on land since the aerodynamic functions of winglets mean that wings can be shorter, which in turn means that aircraft— according to Wikipedia—can better adhere to "operational considerations that limit the allowable wingspan (e.g., available width at airport gates)."

No less an authority than Bill Nye (the Science Guy)—a former Boeing engineer—has penned thoughts on aircraft winglets. "Today, planes have composite plastic winglets," he explains in his recent book on evolution. They are the result of "countless hours of research and development, [as well as] management decisions, engineering analysis, and fabricators' skill." Small but mighty, the winglet mimics structures found in nature (for example: owls' wings). As it turns out, commercial airliners need two of them to fly.

*

On an airplane, only a few passengers at any given time know what's going on outside the windows. Sometimes this is because the shades are down and we are focused on our devices. Sometimes this is because people don't want to look: my friends who are nervous flyers choose aisle seats to avoid vertigo. Personally, I'm one of those people who loves to stare out the window. But even I admit that on the ground, if you're squeamish about big planes in small spaces, it's best to close the shades when at LGA, or perhaps take a nap.

Hardly five minutes after Southwest 449 pushed back from the gate, I jolted from my pre-takeoff snooze: there was a bump, followed by a creak and groan, and the whole plane skittered with locked wheels as though it were sliding on ice. It was an odd sensation, and questionable. I jolted upright as the woman behind me spewed choice words under her breath, concluding: "It's the WING!"

Flight attendants from the back rang the front as the plane braked to a halt. At first neither the pilots (who presumably had been looking forward from the cockpit) nor the flight attendants (who were focused on getting cell phones turned off inside the plane) seemed to know exactly what happened.

But we, on the left side of the plane in front of the wing, had a great view. There on the ground in the drizzle of a New York December lay a forlorn chunk of our wing: a winglet. DING! It looked like a giant Grinch had come to ruin Christmas in Whoville, sating his sadistic gluttony by taking a huge bite out of composite plastic attached to our plane.

Thirty feet below, grounds crews gestured furiously to each other and waved down the pilots. One man picked up the forlorn, chomped winglet (roughly the size of an oversized sandwich-board advertisement) and hauled it somewhat aimlessly across the tarmac—where does one put part of a plane that's fallen off? Other grounds-crew members dialed 911 or 311, the Port Authority hotline, or whomever assesses fault for this kind of thing. Surely *someone* was calling the insurance companies.

Onboard, malcontented murmurs signaled the rising passenger awareness that we were not, in fact, going anywhere anytime soon. Cell phones buzzed and Tweets—unlike the airplane—flew.

The antics on the ground below eventually involved several emergency trucks plus an ambulance, though no one was hurt. Adding to the effect, a bald man in a full-body silver jumpsuit directed traffic and growled directions on a walkie-talkie. We deplaned onto the tarmac as a flight attendant announced with only slight twinge of irony that we should take all of our belongings, "as we will not be returning to this aircraft." (Indeed.) Onto the stair car we clambered; into the buses we streamed; and that's when the *New York Times* called.

A reporter friend had seen my Tweets and passed them on, since news outlets were primed for Christmas-travel drama, and this fit the bill: budget airline at LGA loses part of wing! Port Authority on the case!

Surrounded by yapping dogs and texting passengers, happy to be off a newly defective aircraft but facing down the prospect of spending Christmas apart from family, I described the affair as a "fender bender of the plane variety." Surely we'd all rather lose a wing(let) on the ground than in the air. News channels cued up photos from passengers' Tweets to broadcast around the nation, and we, the foiled travelers, returned to the special purgatory of Concourse B.

Southwest bought us all "free" cookies, gave us flight vouchers, and arranged for another plane to serve as Flight 449 later that afternoon. (Again apparently without a sense of the ironic, the gate agent admonished: "All of our flights are full until next year. So I do advise you to take this one.") Meanwhile people did their best to muster either cheer or tolerance. A gate agent offered $25 vouchers to anyone who'd sing carols over the announcement system (a drawling mother-daughter duo won the prize). Shortly thereafter, a La Guardia-sponsored barbershop quartet appeared with a temporary staging set, to serenade the concourse with more Christmas carols. Sleigh ride!

Like I said: in New York, you put up with a bit of the unexpected in order to achieve your goals.

Only later did details of the collision come to light, though in the moment our pilot had suggested (with discernible annoyance) that grounds crews may have crossed signals. It seemed that as Southwest 449 taxied to the runway and passed another concourse, an American Airlines flight was directed to back out of its gate. And despite the "operational" advantage granted by winglets (namely, shorter wings to better navigate cozy airports), the fact is that when one plane backs into another, something's got to give. In this case, it was the Southwest plane (out of service, due to broken winglet) and the American Airlines passengers (out of luck, since they were delayed nearly twelve hours).

La Guardia that day was a microcosm of NYC in more ways than one. Crammed together, the unexpected became the norm. With holiday travel plans foiled, people were generally decent to one another. The infrastructure of the airport worked: the crews kept us safe, the airline took care of us, and even that grimy, beleaguered Concourse B made room for us.

Plus, we learned that "taxiing" is spelled with two "i's" —yes, just like skiing, but much less fun. Certainly we all now know what a winglet is. Perhaps most surprising is the fact that we arrived in Denver on the same day that we left New York: determined, even if fraying a bit at the edges, and with our luggage in tow. DING!

Airplane Docufictions

Harold Jaffe

Vodka

A man swallowed a liter of top-shelf brand vodka rather than surrender it to airport personnel (who themselves would drink it after hours).

New regulations designed to obstruct terrorism (which the US has in fair part provoked) prohibit passengers from carrying quantities of liquid onto aircraft (does that apply equally to first-class passengers?).

Informed at a security check that he would have to relinquish the vodka or pay a hefty fee to have his carry-on bag checked as cargo, the man chugged the liquor down on the spot, passed out, died.

Official cause of death: *global nausea.*

Undead

A ninety-one-year-old male has been refused flight out of Liverpool's Ringo Starr Airport because he was dead.

The old dead male, in a wheelchair, wearing sunglasses, was delivered to the gate by two middle-aged females.

Airport staff became suspicious while patting him down and noting his lack of body warmth.

Fat Flyers

Air France denied reports that it planned an additional charge for overweight passengers unable to fit into a single seat.

Instead, the national carrier said that from Feb 1, overweight passengers who chose to purchase an extra seat for comfort would get their money back on flights that were not fully booked.

Previously an airline spokesperson said grossly fat flyers will have to pay 75 percent of the cost of a second seat (the full price excluding tax and surcharges) on top of the full price for the first, insisting the decision was for "safety, not esthetic," reasons.

Swallow

An al-Qaeda suicide bomber blew himself up while severely wounding a Saudi prince in Jeddah.

The bombing left people wondering how one of the most-wanted al-Qaeda operatives in Saudi Arabia could get so close to the princely head of counter-terrorism to explode himself and mutilate the prince.

The answer is the explosive was *inside* the bomber's body; he swallowed it.

Western forensic experts are profoundly worried that this deadly new tactic will influence other terrorists; if so, it will render traditional airport-security metal detectors useless.

The best near-term option might be redoubling the emphasis on racial profiling.

Things to Do

Find work as a baggage handler for a major airliner.

Secretly rummage through lost or delayed luggage.

Collect female hair from brushes, combs, intimate wear.

Bag the hair in transparent plastic, label it.

Encode your fantasies of the hair-owner's most intimate gestures on your smart phone.

Skinks

Feds apprehended a man who strapped twenty-two live lizards to his chest to get through customs at LAX.

The thirty-nine-year-old was returning from Australia when in a routine strip-down agents found four geckos, seven monitor lizards and eleven skinks fastened to his body.

The lizards' estimated value: $18,000.

The Great Privilege

Anne Gisleson

In the summer of 2012, I was invited to Tokyo to participate in a disaster symposium. Scholars from all over the world were comparing reconstruction efforts following Hurricane Katrina and the BP oil spill in south Louisiana and the 3-11 earthquake, tsunami and nuclear meltdowns in eastern Japan. Though by then I was weary of our homegrown disasters here in New Orleans, I was interested to hear about how the other side of the globe was coping with theirs. Also, my husband and I had never been to Asia and the university in Tokyo was paying for the flight and hotel room.

After a six-hour layover at LAX, we finally boarded our Malaysia Airlines flight and I felt my first inner jolt of the foreign. The stewards and stewardesses helping people find their seats and fit carry-on bags into overhead compartments were stunning. The women wore fitted, collarless floor-length uniforms with purple and pink flowers generously arranged against a teal lattice pattern. Three-quarter sleeves, discreet slits in the skirts. Their dark glossy hair in perfect up-dos or sharp sloping bobs. The men wore deep-teal suits with white shirts and teal ties. The crew's every gesture was great to watch, lessening the tedium of takeoff preparation.

We had barely reached cruising altitude when a stewardess, in all her formal, floral exuberance, came down the aisles bearing a tray of *free beer*, Singha, Tiger, Sapporo, Asahi, which immediately transported us not only to another hemisphere but to another century of more gracious air travel. Between the free beer, the melatonin and my husband's shoulder, these next 11 hours over the Pacific were going to fly by. In the middle of the night I accidentally spilled a bottle of water and a handsome, concerned steward in his teal suit cleaned it up and brought me a new one, apologizing as though he had caused it. With this warm and lovely crew, we crossed over the international dateline and into the future, losing a day before arriving in Tokyo.

At the conference we relived, shared, theorized and analyzed our various individual and collective disasters, both natural and human-made, and how communities negotiate the aftermath, move forward. We explored a city that had rebuilt itself over and over in the face of destruction. With no real zoning in place, over the decades Tokyo had developed and was still developing in a chaotic accumulation that seemed endless, cranes saluting on the skyline surrounding our hotel in Shibuya.

By the end of the trip, the exclamation mark vibrating in my head all week was starting to wilt. We were worn down by the great privilege of travel, the great privilege of living. Back in the Narita airport, since we couldn't exchange our coins for dollars we stacked our remaining Yen into little columns, and exchanged them for Asahi beers. We drank in a facsimile of a Japanese noodle bar, like most airport eateries a depressing parody of travel that helps loosen your grip on whatever extraordinary experience you've just had. Eases you back into the mundane. After ordering one Asahi too many, we lost track of time and ended up running through the terminal, hitting a gift shop to spend the last of the errant Yen on more presents for our kids, anything with Japanese characters would do, a mini canister of Pringles, a key chain with Sargent Frog hugging the Tokyo Tower. Standing in the gangway waiting to board, I could see two Malaysia Airlines stewardesses at the end of the dim tunnel of shifting, burdened passengers, their beautiful uniforms and smiles. I was looking forward to spending the next half-day in their company.

Two years later, when hearing about each of the Malaysia Airlines disasters, my first thoughts were of the stewardesses and stewards. The pattern on those uniforms filled my mind's eye with a vibrancy I couldn't reconcile with their fate. All that disappeared beauty and graciousness. Since my memory almost always mangles color, shapes, names, events, I thought maybe it was embellishing those uniforms, transforming them into something more glorious than they were. But when I googled "Malaysia Airlines stewardess uniforms," I couldn't believe how accurately I'd recalled them. The colors, the rosettes, the slim cut, all true. Then, scrolling through the images, not knowing whether any of those smiling women had been on those downed flights, I came across a picture of one of the uniform dresses, on the debris field of flight MH-17. It looked perfectly intact, as though it had been carefully draped over the rocky Ukrainian countryside like a flag.

From the Cockpit

Jack Saux

This story dates back to the 1970s, so all statutes of limitations have expired and airline procedures have changed. In the pre-9/11 era, occasionally "bomb threats" could be traced to the last passenger to arrive at the aircraft.

A businessman, running late for his flight, would make a call to the airline reservation system, mention the word "bomb" and hang up. The airline would be forced to take a delay to run safety checks allowing the tardy passenger to make his flight. After several arrests/investigations this activity stopped.

I was a new captain on the airline. We were sitting at the gate in a DC-9 when the agent ran down the jetway and from a distance yelled, "Captain, call Operations."

The fact that he ran was our first clue. Calling from a distance was the second.

I tuned the radio to the company frequency and made the call. "Ops, Delta 123. What's up?"

"Stand by, Delta 123. You may have a bomb threat."

"May?"

"Right, we're checking it out and will get right back to you."

The passengers had already been placed on board. "Be quick."

A long two or three minutes passed.

"Yep, it's you."

"No problem, I will get the people off the bird and back into the terminal." I tried to put on my calm pilot voice.

"You can't do that, Captain. You have to wait for a senior agent to come to your gate and make the announcement."

Heck of a thing to do during a situation like that but the co-pilot and I looked at each other and laughed. I keyed the mike and asked if we had to wait too. This call was not answered.

I made an announcement telling my passengers that I felt certain this was a prank and advised them to take their time, gather their carry-on luggage, and deplane through the forward door. I then told them while there was no need to panic or rush, expeditious movement would be appreciated as I could not leave until they did.

There was no bomb and we survived.

*

On one flight into New Orleans, we lowered the landing gear on approach as usual. But the nose gear did not indicate down and locked. We broke out of the pattern and headed for Lake Pontchartrain. I made an announcement to the people that we had an indication that the nose gear did not function normally.

"Gear unsafe" is not a cool thing to say to passengers.

I advised them that we would be circling over the lake to attempt to resolve the indication. Again, note we did not say "resolve the problem."

Well, we could not get the damn light to go from red to green. We declared an emergency and headed for the runway. I told the passengers that while the little light in the cockpit did not say so, I felt certain that the nose gear was down and locked. "I mention this because as we land you will see lots of airport vehicles with flashing lights nearby in case we need assistance."

I did not say "fire trucks" as this is a bad phrase.

"But just to be doubly safe, I will hold the nose up longer than normal and will wait until we are going real slow before I lower it to the runway."

There was nothing to gain by saying that below seventy knots the elevator was no longer effective and the nose would slam to the runway.

Well, I was right, everything worked normally. As the people were getting off the aircraft, my co-pilot and I stood in the doorway thanking them for selecting our airline.

Two nuns came to the door and grabbed my hand, thanking me.

I told them that if I had known they were on board I would have told the rest of the passengers we had absolutely nothing to worry about.

All the people were off the aircraft and the co-pilot and I were getting our flight kits and suitcases out of the cockpit when the agent approached.

"Smooth, you all," he said with a smile.

I nodded.

"Yep," he said, "two nuns came up to me and asked if they could exchange their return-flight tickets for bus tickets."

The Taste of Guilt

Alethea Kehas

Each summer when I was a child, my sister and I would fly 3000 miles across the country to visit a place my mother was trying to forget. We drove from our home in New Hampshire to fly out of Boston's Logan Airport, stopping midway to change planes, then landing at our destination about nine hours after we began. At Portland International Airport, my sister and I were welcomed by the family we had left behind when we were four and six. Sometimes cousins, aunts, and uncles would be there to greet us, and always our grandparents and birthfather were present. Each person waiting behind the gate wore the face of happiness and reunion, while my sister and I struggled with our bags and the sensation of a distance too quickly spanned.

With the speed of the airplane, our bisected world merged. Boundaries turned foggy and dissolved. The split halves collided and emitted sparks. New Hampshire didn't seem to belong in Oregon. Oregon didn't belong in New Hampshire. Where, I wondered, did I belong?

A year could not be condensed into two weeks, I soon came to realize. Birthdays and holidays were celebrated with absences. The void greater on the East Coast than on the West, for we were only two people. Life, I saw in the milestones of my cousins, went on without me and my sister. At home in New Hampshire, my sister and I struggled to navigate our way into a new family of step-cousins, aunts, uncles, and grandparents, and when we returned to Oregon, we tried to reclaim a space that seemed to get smaller every summer.

It confused me to return each year to the state of my birth. When I felt happiness swimming with my cousins and eating my grandmother's dried apples while the sun evaporated the water from our bathing suits, I also felt guilt. Should I still love these people my mother no longer spoke to? Where did I fit in this place she refused to revisit?

Often, the only thing that made sense to me was the weight-lessness of the flights. In the air my anxiety would dissolve and I would marvel at the capacity of the clouds to absorb the body of the plane without protest, and the way the earth below patched itself together like a bedspread. Like my grandmother's afghan.

In the air I belonged to no one. I was, in essence, free. When the pilot turned off the seatbelt sign I roamed about the cabin in search of the tiny bathrooms, where I would sequester myself inside the humming walls and marvel at the force of the toilet, then wash my hands in the doll-sized sink.

Back at my seat, my sister would be waiting for me, ready to play another game of "spit," with our slippery new deck of cards. Although younger, I liked to fancy myself the braver sister. Certainly I was the only one who dared to eat everything on the meal tray the stewardess would kindly set down on our waiting tables.

It was during a flight to Oregon, when I was nine, that I had my first taste of meat. The stewardess had just served me and my sister our trays, each a complete country breakfast of scrambled eggs, sausage and toast (no one had told her we were vegetarians). My sister, immediately alarmed by the links of pork nestled beside our eggs, warned me not to touch the glistening meat. But, she also made the mistake of going to the bathroom before our breakfasts were finished.

While my sister was in the lavatory, I stared hard at those brown steaming links. And the smell, well, it was too much to bear. My stomach grumbled its plea, and my mouth dripped with moisture. More than anything else at that moment, I wanted those sausages. By the time my sister had returned, not only were mine gone, but hers had disappeared as well into my satisfied stomach. My sister, when she saw the missing links from our trays, turned to me in horror.

"You ate the sausages!" she cried out in alarm, as though I had just picked and consumed not one, but four, poisonous mushrooms. In a way, I suppose, I had.

"Mom and Dad are going to kill you!"

"I don't care," I replied. "They were delicious!"

Ridden by guilt, my sister confessed my sin two weeks later. She held the secret of my crime just until we made it through the arrival gates and into the arms of our waiting mother and stepfather. Instead of the cries of alarm she had anticipated though, our parents erupted into laughter.

"How'd they taste?" my stepfather asked me with a wink of his eye.

Eating Fish on a Plane

Aaron Gilbreath

My plane from Oregon landed at Narita Airport on the evening of January 1st. A woman in the seat behind me wore a paper SARS mask on her mouth and a pink eye mask with the phrase "Sweet Dreams" written in jewels. Delta Airlines served Sencha tea in place of Lipton. Only hours into the new year, everything was new—except the beef stroganoff. The stroganoff Delta served tasted like the subpar, microwavable variety I'd eaten as a kid in Phoenix, Arizona, only here in smaller portions and with more leathery beef.

Why Delta was serving bad versions of American-family staples to people who favored Japanese green tea was beyond me. Even as an American, I avoided those staples for healthier items, which on my flight back from Japan included fish: thin, moist slices of lightly pickled saury, known as *sanma* in Japanese, draped over a pressed roll of chewy sushi rice. I bought the *sanma* in Tokyo's Ikebukuro train station that morning. The best part: no one on the plane said anything. In America, people would eye you disapprovingly if you ate pungent fish in a confined space. In Japan, you're not going to "offend" anyone for eating fish like this. I know. I'd done this years ago on a flight back from Alaska, when the smoked halibut my mom and I bought on the docks in Seward was too mouth-watering to keep in our bag during the six-hour flight home. We're Jews. Smoked fish is our heritage. We had to eat it. But when we opened the two Ziploc bags, the smell filled the cabin. The man beside us shot us a look before shifting in his seat. I'm sure nearby passengers scrunched their noses. The smell probably made others groan. We didn't care. We savored every moist smoky bite of that halibut and licked our briny fingers when it was gone. On the flight back from Japan alone, I did the same thing, and I felt no guilt.

Passengers readied movies on their laptops. Others leaned their chairs back to sleep. I laid my sushi on the tiny tray table beside Patrick Smith's book *Japan: A Reinterpretation*. Tokyo Bay passed outside my window, as the setting sun cast the ocean and last spits of land in a liquid amber. And, slowly, I ate. The rice tasted of sweet vinegar. The oily filets melted in my mouth. The stewardess offered me a croissant egg-and-cheese sandwich, but I declined. "Something to drink?" she said. I said, "Green tea and orange juice, please." I set the Minute Maid beside the cup of Sencha and nibbled the fish. I didn't want to finish; the empty container would only prove that my three-week trip to Japan was over. Although I bought *sanma* for sustenance, I ate to extend my visit. As long as I had fish, I still had Japan, even over the open ocean. But in nine hours the plane would deposit me back in a country that favored overcooked beef to fresh seafood, this, the country of my birth, where my family and destiny and childhood memories lay, but where I often felt so gravely out of place.

I Was Not the Stewardess of His Porno Movies

Amanda Pleva

"Now boarding all rows for Flight 920, with service to Tokyo Narita."

I stared longingly at the neighboring gate as I waited with my crew for the pilots to arrive. Tokyo was my favorite city, with its frenetic pace, its history, food, and culture. It was much more alluring to me than my upcoming overnight in New York City, which is thirty miles from where I was born and raised. I daydreamed about being on that crew instead, and having a Suntory Whiskey-fueled karaoke session at the sleepy hotel bar outside the city. I studied the blank faces of the queued up passengers. If I were on that line, I thought, I'd be much more alive-looking. It was impossible for me to comprehend how one could have such a ho-hum countenance when a city such as Tokyo was on the other end of the journey.

My envious gaze was broken by a man walking between me and the Tokyo flight to throw out his coffee cup. He met my eyes and smiled broadly. Before my brain could muster a reaction, he disappeared. I'd attempted to smile back, but my brain hadn't returned from Japan in time to catch him. He was attractive, in his early thirties, with thick-rimmed black glasses. I wouldn't have been bowled over, but his smile had caught my attention enough to scan the crowd looking for him before I turned around to board the plane.

The flight from LAX to JFK was quick and uneventful. I was disappointed that I hadn't seen him on board, but was by no means heartbroken. I'd envisioned us engaging in a banal conversation while he waited for the lavatory; maybe comparing New York and Los Angeles, maybe about his work, or he'd ask about mine. Instead, perhaps he was aboard the Tokyo flight, well on his way over the Pacific Ocean as I now bordered the Atlantic. I stood in the front galley with the captain and another flight attendant as the passengers deplaned and we said our goodbyes. I was once again off in a daydream as I was handed a folded over piece of music-composition paper. I looked up to see the same smile I'd been hoping to reciprocate. My face turned hot as I took the note and happily shoved it in my pocket. As he exited the plane, the captain and my coworker looked at me and grinned.

"So," asked Colleen, my coworker. "Are you gonna open it or what?"

I pulled it back out of my pocket, studied it for a moment, and then ducked into the corner of the galley. I hid behind the bulkhead as the rest of the passengers left and unfolded the paper.

It was not a note but a drawing. It was in pencil, very detailed and carefully shaded. His name—Adam—and phone number were written along the right edge. The drawing was of me…from the back.

I couldn't immediately react. I had so many questions! Why a drawing in the first place? We'd been in an aircraft together for nearly six hours, and he'd made no attempts to talk to me. And why did he draw my back? Was this an artistic rendering, or was it to confirm that he had noticed my butt? Was the advance romantic or merely sexual? And how hadn't I seen him the whole flight? I called Colleen over. "You have *got* to see this."

"Is that supposed to be—"

"Yup."

"Whoa. That's just weird."

"It's definitely weird, but at the same time, maybe it's kind of flattering? Eric, what's your take?" I handed the paper to the captain. He began to laugh uncontrollably. I wanted to as well, but I couldn't figure out if it was out of giddiness or amusement.

Maybe both.

"I saw him working away on this the whole flight, but I didn't know that it was you!" Colleen said. "I would have warned you."

"I don't know. Maybe I'll text him. That's just impersonal enough to remain noncommittal. I don't know yet if I want to actually talk to this guy yet."

Colleen looked concerned. "Really? You're interested?"

I thought for a second. "I guess I'll find out soon enough."

As we waited outside in the chilly New York air for the hotel van to pick us up, I looked at the number on the drawing and entered the number into my phone. I made a couple edits of the message I was going to send him. I hesitated for a moment before hitting "send." The message read:

Hey, it's Amanda, the flight attendant. I'd noticed you too, in LAX. Was hoping to get a chance to talk to you. Maybe next Saturday we can get together, will be back in NYC then.

I felt foolish as I awaited a reply. One came not too long afterward, and it was a very short confirmation of our date to happen the following week. I showed more friends the masterpiece, and their reactions were as mixed as mine had been. Some adamantly advised against the date, some insistent that I go. I waffled between the two, but stayed with my decision to meet him, albeit more reluctantly as Saturday approached.

I asked him meet me at my old haunt in the Lower East Side, a bar near my old apartment, to be on familiar ground. We didn't talk much during the week after the flight, and when I'd gotten a voicemail message from him that day, he sounded awkward and unconfident. I'd lost interest a bit. As my cab pulled up, I felt my first slight pangs of anxiety, and hoped he would more closely resemble the Adam of LAX than the Adam in JFK.

I walked in to find him smiling smugly at a table in the empty bar. He gave me playful grief for arriving late, as my flight had been delayed due to bad weather. We sat down. I immediately felt less anxious but more uncertain of what I'd walked into. He went to the bar and returned with a can of PBR for himself and a pint of Old Speckled Hen for me. He sat down in the booth.

"So, a flight attendant! You must be pretty busy," he asked with a smirk. I felt uneasy.

"Yes," I said, "I fly full-time, and I have a two year-old son as well, so I'm pretty busy at home, too." I was careful to watch for a reaction. He paused for a moment, and stared contemplatively at the wall.

"I'm trying to picture you pregnant right now, and it's pretty hot." I winced, and officially called it: Adam was creepy.

"Oh. Well, thanks. So. Where do you live in Brooklyn?" I gulped as much beer as possible.

He lived in Williamsburg, Brooklyn—that was, when not on tour. He was a very skilled musician who played live shows with an aging rock group from the 1970s, which were filling Indian casinos and county fairs instead of arenas now. I asked him the general "touring musician" roster of questions; he asked me the "flight attendant" ones. I was still not enjoying myself, especially as he kept trying to squeeze innuendo into the conversation. He went to the bathroom; I considered leaving. He returned with another Old Speckled Hen for me. Damn.

I stayed and tolerated the last of the date, and announced that I needed to head back to my hotel. He unfortunately told me he was catching the same train back home as I was taking back to the airport. As the J train rolled on through Brooklyn, he began bragging about his method for hiding hash in his luggage en route home from the band's European tour. He looked in my eyes hopefully, but he began to get the message. I was looking for a date that night; I was not the stewardess of his porno movies, and he had played the wrong card. His face completely changed.

"Well, I hope I get to see you again the next time you fly through New York," he said meekly as he stood up. His stop was next.

"Thanks for the beer," I said with finality. I returned his hug weakly.

The doors closed behind him. I immediately felt immense relief. I fished my earbuds from the pocket of my coat and sunk back in the seat. The train rattled on to JFK, and I tried not to fall asleep.

In-Flight Mistress

Roger Sedarat

After seventeen years of marriage, I had a little affair with my wife. Because it happened on an airplane, to this day I find flying especially erotic. On this particular family trip I had arranged the seating for our various connecting flights from Newark to Dallas-Fort Worth, then from there to San Antonio, where we were taking our two young sons to visit family. In making our travel plans, my wife noticed that I had reserved seats for her and our five-year-old one row ahead of me and our three-year-old.

"That sucks there aren't seats for us all in a row," she said. "Why don't you take the one in front this time?"

"No, I actually planned it like this," I replied. "And I *insist* that you sit there," I added, plopping Theo, the three-year-old, in the middle seat next to my coat.

"What are you talking about?" she asked (a little edgy from the travel) as she sat down and leaned over the seat behind her to talk with us.

"Well," I admitted, "I have a little thing for this dark-haired woman sitting in front of me, a hot single mom. I want to look at her on the flight, and if I'm feeling a connection, maybe...you know...hit on her a little."

At first she kind of rolled her eyes, mentally checking the box of the category for weird husband (and I consistently score high on that survey, according to her). That was the wife I've known all too well and with whom I've already had five little fights on the way to the airport about directions and why she won't let me drive because of her getting carsick.

A second later, however, things changed. There was a slight shift in her reaction after initially blowing me off. In retrospect, I'm sure such slight shifts often occur in our interactions, but I'm usually too frazzled in our routine with the kids to notice.

For a split second, she became the woman of my dreams. It happened when she got up to take her son (and most of this fantasy involves me momentarily disclaiming the kid with her) on the walk down the aisle to the potty. She paused for a brief moment before me. I looked her up and down, really sexy-like. If it were a business environment, I'd be risking sexual harassment. This cracked her up a little, and I sensed I had a real chance with her.

Later in the trip, before we reached San Antonio, things got even more enticing. I finally summoned the strength to ask her if she liked the book she was reading, where she was headed, and all the usual banter. We both sort of broke out of character, along with our kids, when I asked her son what his name was and made an attempt to introduce my son to the other boy and his mom. The whole family got the collective joke, trying to sustain it with more questions as we kept cracking ourselves up. Fortunately, things fell back into place when I asked about her earrings (she said her ex-husband had bought them for her). I then started to play a little with her hair.

Of course my ultimate desire in the moment was for the first time becoming a member of the mile-high club, taking her into one of the two, cleaner, compartmental bathrooms and losing myself in sex with her positioned on the edge of that metallic sink (which, like a gentleman, I'd first wipe down). I even wanted at some point in our frenzied love-making for an irate flight attendant to have figured out what we were up to, perhaps because we'd fail to return to our seats near landing or during turbulence after the fasten seatbelt sign had come on. We'd eventually emerge and start the return to our seats, relieved and exhausted, her hair messed up and both of us continuing to arrange our clothing as we walked down the aisle, making all of the other passengers, who at best reluctantly caught up on some lame movie they'd decided not to watch at home, extremely jealous.

I knew the impossibility of such a scenario, especially with a kid beside each of us in a window seat. Even so, it was my once-in-a-lifetime, ultimate in-flight movie. I knew that she knew I was screening it in my head the whole time as I made things a little more romantic, ordering a dark chocolate candy bar for her from the flight attendant in hush tones and instructing that it be delivered to the lady one row ahead of me. My wife mouthed the words "thank you" and blew me a very hot kiss. She then even more clandestinely snuck a couple of squares to our son beside her, hoping not to kill the mystery with the mundane engagement of parenting.

Much later that night, in the guest bathroom at my mother's house after our kids finally fell asleep, she surprisingly turned my whole constructed intrigue around on me. While brushing her teeth with her pajamas on, she started asking how my flight went today, and whether I met anybody on the plane.

"You wouldn't believe this dark-haired woman I sat behind," I told her, as she put lotion on her face.

"What was her name?" she asked.

"Janette," I told her.

"What was she like?"

"Smoking hot." I said, starting to brush my teeth. "I have to say she was the sexiest, most seductive woman I've ever met."

"Wow," said my wife, with a certain tone of ennui, as if casually commenting upon a mildly interesting event I'd tell her about work. "Was she into you?" she asked, now brushing her hair.

"I think so," I said, "but it's always hard to tell."

"Did you take her in the bathroom to...you know...join the mile-high club?" she asked, as we both peered in at our sleeping kids next door to the guest room.

"No," I said, holding the guest room door open for her, "but I really wanted to."

"You should have tried," she said casually.

We both read in silence from the books that we hadn't touched on our journey, and after a few minutes, kissed each other goodnight, turned out the bedside lamps, and went to sleep.

Pretension

Kim Chinquee

On the plane to Mexico, the woman next to me said she was going to find Jesus. She bounced her boy, a toddler, and said Maine weather made her evil. She smiled at me. Her baby laughed.

Looking out the window, I wanted to put an arm out. The clouds seemed beneath us. The woman leaned in and she asked if I believed.

I looked at her red lipstick, noticed a mark on her tooth like a cross, and I told her I believed in a lot of things.

Like what? she said.

I said, I'm going on vacation.

She said she'd been a cheat. She said she was clean now. She told me something saved her.

I told her that was good. I got a book out, one I'd written, only because it was the only one with me. It was mostly about women with problems with their partners, who'd been abused by fathers, women who were tough and independent. I opened to a story called Jesus, about a girl whose father was a pastor.

The woman's baby started to cry. She got out a blanket, put him under, drew him to her. She said to me, Excuse me.

My son had done the cover, a portrait of a face with pouty lips and dark eyes. The book was called Pretension, the title of a story about a woman on a plane with her toddler.

When the attendant came around, I ordered a Bloody Mary. The woman next to me said she wanted nothing. As I sipped, I looked at my watch, wondering if my boyfriend had arrived yet. He was meeting me at the place he'd booked the month before, the trip a gift to me because he said he loved me. We'd be fishing, sailing, bathing at a beach house.

When I finished my drink, the woman grabbed my hand and

told me that God loved me. I was ready for a nap then.

As I closed my eyes, she sneezed, and I said, Bless you.

Air Prayer

Nicole Sheets

I swigged cough syrup as discreetly as I could, in a way that I hoped seemed all business rather than recreational.

I stowed a roll of square Halls lozenges in my jacket pocket for easy access during the flight. I didn't want to be that tubercular-sounding bitty that you shoot the stinkeye because you know she is going to infect you, she's going to ruin your trip or wreck you once you get home.

But I was on my third rapid-fire cough drop, and I couldn't stop rattling. The more I tried to suppress the cough, the more my throat rollicked and bucked.

I was in the aisle seat, my favorite. The woman in the window seat, JoEllen, had discerned early on that I'm a teacher. She'd seemed friendly enough, but I buried myself in my book right away.

"You must like to read," she'd said. There was no one in the seat between us. JoEllen let me stash my overstuffed backpack in front of our empty middle seat. I discreetly scissor-kicked in all my unfathomable legroom.

And I coughed. I dug through my pack for a water bottle.

On a plane, there's a right moment to break the seal of conversation. I'm all for the polite greeting as you sit down, an apology if necessary as you grope for the end to insert in your seatbelt buckle, a self-deprecating remark as you splash coffee and fumble for napkins to swab it up.

The best moment to talk with your neighbor is often when the captain announces that we're nearing our final destination and the flight attendants will come through for one final cleanup. When you stow and lock your tray table, you know that no matter how weird the conversation gets, it's not going to last that long.

JoEllen and I were not yet close to our final destination.

If I closed my eyes, my cough relented a little, as though I could focus my mind's eye on my throat.

JoEllen made her move. Clearly, I had surrendered my unwavering focus on my book.

"What kind of school do you teach at?" she asked. I told her.

"So you're a Christian?"

Yes, I said, I am, though in my head I also inserted imaginary asterisks, like:

*probably not the kind of Christian you mean
*not the kind with a Jesus fish on her car
*more the kind with a decently stocked liquor cabinet
*who struggles to freshen her potty mouth.

"When you said you were a professor, I didn't know," JoEllen explained. "You all have some wild beliefs sometimes." I like wild beliefs, but I didn't say anything. I just waited for the Halls vapors to soothe me.

"Would you mind if I prayed for your cough?" she asked.

Sure.

"Would you mind if I laid a hand on your shoulder?"

OK.

JoEllen requested my healing and relief: "We speak the name of Jesus into her bronchial system." I pictured the letters J-E-S-U-S, part Sunday School craft and part antibiotic, coursing through my lungs.

JoEllen didn't speak in tongues, which both disappointed and relieved me.

I grew up in a family that would often pray out loud, at the Pizza Hut, say, as the server stands there with the extra napkins you asked for: "We thank you for this food, Lord, in the name of your precious Son Jesus…"

My cough didn't vanish. Doves failed to soar from the seatback pocket in front of me. But JoEllen's prayer did comfort me in my affliction.

She said that she and her husband traveled in their RV for seven years before they decided to retire in Montana. They've been trying to sell the RV for a while. "God runs our lives," JoEllen said. "We must be hanging on to it for a reason."

They chose their retirement town in Montana because of a church there with a food and clothing pantry and a wood ministry. The church bids on parcels of land and cuts the dead trees, then splits, bundles and delivers the firewood to people who need it. I had to admit that a church with its own logging truck is pretty badass.

There was nothing smug about JoEllen. I liked her. Still she triggered the anxieties of my Evangelical heyday. What if you're the only Bible some people ever read? Are you proclaiming the gospel of Jesus Christ at all times? At best, it was exhausting. At worst, maddening.

From time to time I run across students who use everything they write, every comment they make to point explicitly to their Lord and Savior. I want to honor their point of view even as I freak out a little on the inside. Don't pull me back into that vortex of worry! Lighten up, I want to say to them.

JoEllen didn't put her inquisition beams on me, her doctrinal brights, and for that I was grateful. JoEllen seemed plenty light.

You Are Sitting in a Chair in the Sky

Timothy Morton

Air travel brings up a lot of strong emotions, most of them negative: boredom, scorn, pride, paranoia, anger, loneliness, stupor, smugness, anxiety, sadness, humiliation, tenderness, aggression, fear, frustration, sluggishness, exhaustion. Thus air travel is the ideal fuel for anyone who wastes most of her or his life doing meditation.

The meditator does not regard negative emotions as a turn off or as a sign that things are going wrong. Rather, they are the meat of your mind, far tastier than anything that is served on either side of the flimsy transparent curtain that separates the smug from the humiliated.

In particular, the basic emotion of living humans is anxiety—meditators agree with Heidegger that this is the bedrock. You should thank heaven and earth every time it comes up, like a flight attendant offering you a choice of chicken or pasta.

That all starts with the uncanny realization that this is not my beautiful home town, this is not my beautiful car—this is a slightly crappy airporter at four a.m. driving through the neighborhood I never go to in my life, absurd vocoding singers machinating on the radio, confusing street lights and colors, the slight sickness of an unfamiliar person's driving.

This feeling of basic anxiety is the meditator's best friend. As soon as you hit it, you should rejoice—you rediscovered the one emotion that never lies! Greet it like an old friend. Put that iPhone down. Feel it: it kinda sucks to be sentient, doesn't it?

An added bonus is that one gets some time with somewhat large amounts of anybody at all. We are often too careful about who we associate with and modern society encourages this in various ways. Air travel is a wonderful way to experience your idea of his idea of her idea of you, what some call *the social I*. Most people in this culture are way too identified with their social I. Most of the emotions on the list above would be seriously assuaged if we just picked up the habit of dropping our social I once in a while. They might even vanish. An awful lot of what one experiences, the meditator knows, is not genuine: it's just your idea of her idea of his idea...

But perhaps the ultimate prize for the yogi is that plane flight allows most everyone to experience all kinds of fear and panic, mostly around death. People who travel a lot—I travel a reasonable amount I guess—can become quite blasé about this attunement to death. But it's such a precious opportunity to realize that at any moment your skull could pop open at ultra-low pressure, or you could be crushed by millions of tons of water. Or the front of the plane could break open and you would be falling, exposed to thousands of feet of air, revolving, falling.

And you are in no sense in control—a great similarity with going on retreat is that you have to do what others say and sit still. Who ever does that, who isn't a yogini?

Under such conditions, strong emotions arise. You watch a movie and weep at the corniest moments you never dreamed you would shed a tear at. You find food delicious or disgusting, in excess of how you'd taste it on the ground. You see, after you die, after takeoff, you still have your mind. Only it's not quite you anymore. There are a lot of memories, sure. But everything is slightly displaced. I wish I could assure you that it's just a blank void or heavenly choirs. I'm afraid it's going to be much more like a plane ride—without a clear destination.

You see the ground is not just earth, terra firma, but it's your body and it's your world and it's your connection to enlightenment. It's a big mistake to think that enlightenment lies in heavenly space. In that direction, for most people, it becomes a bad trip very quickly. Thank goodness we have ears and greasy fingers and use toilets. The Buddhas' are in your body.

So when you have your body strapped into a chair and shot into space, you have a marvelous opportunity to see how you'll do in the bardo, the after-death state. Most people who are not meditators pass out after they die, because the brilliant clear intensity of the first bardo is just too much. Then they come to in the bardo of dharmata, which is full of grinding, rushing sounds and strong emotions, like being on a plane.

The whole thing, from the fluff in your navel to the furthest reaches of the horizon, is your mind projection. It's you, and it isn't you. That roaring sound of death? That's your basic energy, your basic ignorance. You can't turn it off. You have to just enjoy the ride.

On a plane, you can practice noticing that you are caught in your emotions, then you can bring yourself back to what is really happening. You may not be on Earth but you still have your body. You are sitting in a chair. You are sitting in a chair in the sky.

A few weeks ago I gave meditation instruction to the Occupy UC Davis people, in a geodesic dome. The blue tarp was filled with sunlight. It was perfect—like sitting on a plane.

Exiting a plane is always awesome for a yogi. It's the biggest anticlimax ever.

Anticlimaxes are good. You smile at the way you saw check-in and security and going to the right gate as the Stations of the Cross—or wondered why you so defensively covered your basic fear of death with a blasé sheen. You were simply traveling from A to B. Just like after you die, where you go from one life to the next.

I sometimes think that the bardo of becoming, which is what happens to you if you don't make it in the bardo of dharmata, is like being in Denver International Airport.

"Mr. Quisckhammer, Mr. J. Quisckhammer—Ms. F.E. Ferstle, Ms. F.E. Ferstle—please go to a white courtesy telephone."

It's just an airport. Just like a supermarket is just a building with products in it. Just like a coffin is a box with you in it. Just like being married is just you committed for life to another human. It's only an airport.

I sometimes think that people who travel a lot don't just do it for utilitarian reasons—what a good alibi, right? I believe that they do it because something in air travel seduces them. And behind whatever is seducing them, is their naked mind, as odd and as shocking as a newborn baby.

And as you exit the airport, these strange heightened feelings go away. You put it down to alcohol or high altitude. Everything is perfectly normal, as if nothing had happened, and you have no idea who you really aren't.

God, Please Let Me Fit

Rebecca Renee Hess

I am overweight. Since childhood, size has defined me. Teased, tormented and taunted as a kid because of my butt and belly, adulthood obesity presents a unique set of problems. One of those is flying. I love to travel. I want to visit Paris, Italy, London. I want to be an expatriate. I've read that overseas flights are much stricter when it comes to large passengers so I satiate myself with trips across the country for business.

Before I book my flight, I research. I find articles about Southwest kicking Kevin Smith off a plane because he was "too fat to fly" (catchy phrase). No Southwest. I flew Delta to St. Louis in 2009 and United to Pittsburgh in 2010 and vaguely remember both seatbelts having a bit of leeway tucked discreetly underneath my gut. United it is. With the chairs seventeen inches across and a pitch of thirty-four inches, I take the liberty of booking seats A and C knowing that no solo-traveling stranger wants to sit in-between me and my window-riding companion. I, of course, take the aisle seat.

This year, the annual convention will be in New Orleans. I plan to travel with three friends. Skinny, svelte friends who love me as I am, yet have no idea about the turmoil that dwells in me as I plan to travel. So many people believe weight is a choice, and to some extent, it is. I admit to being a binge eater. To me it feels like a choice, perpetuated. I remember Mark, a fellow third-grader, who used to call me ugly, bird's nest, fatso. The other kids laughed, some of them joined in. I mostly pretended words did not affect me. Except when I threw a desk at Mark and ran out of the classroom crying. High school taught me to hide in plain sight from judgmental peers—to pretend my insecurities did not exist. These lessons help to maintain a standoffish sort of lifestyle in Southern California as an overweight woman. Go ahead and snigger behind your hands! I may ignore you or kick your ass, depending on how far we both are willing to go.

Ready to book, I find that airlines give plus-size passengers the option to purchase a "seatbelt extender" as a precaution against an embarrassing predicament. More embarrassing, though, is the scenario in which one of my friends catches me buckling my extender into the seatbelt.

"God, please let me fit" is my mantra as I buy the non-refundable ticket. Even my office chair is twenty inches across, my rational mind screams as I press the "purchase" link for the $350 round-trip to the Crescent City. Three different airplanes means three seatbelts and three gut-busting experiences.

Just because I'm fat does not mean my weight will affect you, seat neighbor, during a three-hour flight. Flight attendant, I promise not to leak out into the aisle as you roll your metal cart up and down serving stale soda and burnt coffee. Flying is a privilege, I suppose, not a right. From my travel companions I fear scorn, or worse, pity. Still, I don't want to talk about it, I don't want you to help me start an exercise plan, I don't want an operation, I just want to see the world.

Humiliation is a Part of Us All

Greg Keeler

Delta had just absorbed Northwest and I didn't know which gate to check in at when I was returning home from D.C. a couple of summers ago, so I went to Delta. The desk clerks looked at me like I was nuts and said something like, "No, we ain't gotchew here." But then a woman typy-typed for a half minute or so and said, "Well, I guess we do." Since my carry-on looked a lot like my to-be-checked wheely-case, I let them grab my carry-on (for a fifteen-buck baggage fee) and dashed toward security check for the Delta terminal.

When I finally got to the guy who checked my ticket, he said, "You're in the wrong terminal, buddy. Northwest is about a half-mile that way." So I ran and ran, my little *wrong* wheely-case bouncing behind me. When I got to the Northwest terminal security check with a smidgen of time to catch my flight, they jerked my *wrong* wheely-case off of the belt because my white-noise sleep machine looked like something funny in the X-ray; then they started rummaging through my *wrong* stuff.

As I get older, when I travel I get horribly constipated, so, in my *wrong* wheely-case was a big blue enema bulb that was folded up in some underwear. When the security guy lifted the underwear, the enema bulb went flying out onto the terminal floor where I chased it down in front of all of the other passengers waiting in line. Enema bulbs don't roll in a straight line. They sort of bounce then roll in a tight little circle, a motion guaranteed to draw the interest of anyone in the proximity. The security guy's face turned red, but he didn't say anything when I stuffed the enema bulb back into my wheely-case in front of an amused audience.

I barely made my flight to Bozeman, and when I arrived late

that night, my unintentionally checked carry-on wasn't on the plane. I filled out all of the proper forms for lost luggage and assumed that Delta would bring it to my house, which is eight miles from the airport.

They never did.

I went to their on-line site, filled out all the proper forms for lost items, including a $600 camera. A couple of weeks later a woman called and asked me if I had received my luggage yet. I said, "No, but..." and she hung up on me. After another month my wife finally got someone from Delta's baggage-complaints division on the phone. She said she wasn't authorized to give her name but said I should fill out all of the forms again and fax them to a specific number. So I did. Three times.

Two years later, I've never heard back from anyone at Delta. But hey, they don't take responsibility for cameras anyway, and, well, humiliation is a part of us all.

Things They Ran Through the X-Ray

Jason Harrington

Each week, the Transportation Security Administration's Instagram account parades photos of some of the weird, wacky and dangerous things that TSA agents have discovered in carry-on luggage at airports. This is intended to give the impression that the TSA is successfully combating some sort of existential threat to the American way of life, as it purports to be doing with its seven-billion-dollar annual budget.

Much more interesting, however, are the dirty little finds that don't fit into anodyne government accounts of TSA agents' daily experiences. Perhaps the best part of working six years for the TSA was hearing about—and often seeing first-hand—the *truly* crazy things that float across x-ray screens.

At most large airports there is the inevitable story of a TSA officer who has had himself run through the x-ray machine and subsequently been fired for it. At O'Hare airport a friend of mine, a young female officer whom we'll call Savannah, was involved in one such incident in 2010. She was running an x-ray machine on a small vendor checkpoint at O'Hare, 6 alpha, one of the checkpoints the public rarely sees. Vendor checkpoints are used to screen airport employees who have to bring pallets full of goods over to the secure side. The difference between the passenger x-ray machines and the vendor machines is that the latter are much larger, wide enough to accommodate crates of beer and wine, for instance.

Or, in at least one case, a person.

Savannah was on the x-ray machine, and a guy named Blake was on duty as bag-checker. It was slow at 6A, late at night, with little vendor traffic coming through. And so Blake, bored as he was, got the bright idea to actually do what so many TSA officers had only dared speculate about.

"Run me through the x-ray," he told Savannah. He laid down upon the large conveyor belt, urging Savannah to do it.

As she later told me after she'd been fired, Savannah at first laughed at the request, thinking, "This white boy is out of his mind." She refused to click the Forward button. But Blake persisted and, eventually, Savannah gave in.

"He was just an organic mass, a big blur. Besides the badge at least," Savannah told me. It turns out that a male TSA agent looks much like you would expect it to on an x-ray screen: an enormous orange blob with a black blotch for a badge.

Cats, too, show up as reddish clouds on an airport x-ray screen—this I saw many times for myself. How many pets I watched go through the x-ray I cannot say for certain, but I do know that cats far outnumbered dogs. For some reason confused pet-owners tended to think it was alright to send their cats through the x-ray tunnel, possibly because cats are less vocal about things than dogs.

Babies also occasionally ended up on the x-ray belt. I heard vague rumors of babies going all the way through the machine, showing up as little orange blips on some x-ray operator's screen, and I'll tell you, I would not bet against it having happened. But personally, I only saw and heard, first-hand, about close calls. The close-call placement of babies on the x-ray belt usually involved international travelers so perplexed and flustered by the neurotic, 9/11-traumatized nature of American airport security— all the fussing about shoes and commands to get inside full-body scanners and esoteric liquid rules made so little sense—that they were understandably unsure of what they were supposed to do with their babies. Take the baby out of the stroller? Submit it to make sure it contained less than 3.4 ounces of liquids? Taste the baby to prove it wasn't poisonous? American airport security can be pretty baffling to well-traveled Americans, so imagine what it looks like to a first-time flyer from rural Greenland.

Pilots and flight attendants were exempt from the liquids rule, and the amount of alcohol that airline people brought to the checkpoint shocked TSA new-hires without fail. Bottle after bottle of hard liquor, beer and champagne was revealed on our x-ray screens when crew showed up. Most TSA agents, at one point or another, asked the flight crew, "Having some fun tonight, eh?" before adding, in a hopeful tone, "*After* you land the plane and settle in the hotel room, right?"

Finally, I was intrigued by the irrepressible sexual hunger that compels the passengers of this great nation to bring vibrators, dildos and other assorted sex toys aboard the plane with their carry-on luggage. I know the people of this great nation are strong and have within themselves the capacity to overcome irrationality. I know they are capable of being unfazed by the "endless series of political hobgoblins," as Mencken termed them, that the TSA assures people are the cause of peanut-butter confiscations and privacy compromises. I know this due to the fortitude displayed by the passengers who bravely press on, exposing themselves to the risk of having an officer rummage through their bags and pull out large sex toys.

I recall doing a bag check on a man from Detroit, once the auto-making capital of the world. Having been informed by the x-ray operator that there was a bottle of water in the bag, I pulled it out and quickly sensed that something was slightly off. Then, I realized what it was: there was an enormous dildo rubber-banded to it. After a few moments it hit me, spreading over me like a sunrise, beautiful and exhilarating: *He wanted me to have to deal with the dildo.* He did it on purpose. In rubber-banding that dildo to the water bottle he knew we would target, he seemed to say:

"Yes, I have a dildo, federal officer. Even after the horrors of 9/11, I am still alive, full of vitality, love, sex, and, later tonight, that large dildo rubber-banded to the water you are about to confiscate from me. That bottle of water, bought with hard-earned American dollars to replenish my bodily fluids, so as to make me strong and keep this nation's wheels of commerce turning. I want you to see my dildo. To hold it in your hand. To know that I, as well as my fellow passengers, am strong and resilient. That we, the people of this great nation, can, and will, snap back, like that rubber band."

The Great Escape

Stephen Rea

I admit it's ironic. I'm trapped in an airport, the place you go to escape.

I've been stuck in DFW for eleven hours. Best-case scenario, I leave in fifty-five minutes. Worst-case scenario, I could be here for days. The perils of holiday-weekend standby travel...

I've flown a lot. I owned a travel agency for twelve years and visited all seven continents, more than a hundred countries, all fifty united states. I've sipped champagne in First Class above the Atlantic, zipped from New York to London in three hours aboard the Concorde, and I've been whisked around America in a private Lear jet. I've shared planes with Muhammad Ali, Rod Stewart, and Richard Branson, though not all at the same time.

Once a guy died right in front of me in Jakarta airport, less than ten feet away. In the lounge of the Indonesian airline Garuda International, an overweight middle-aged businessman sat opposite me and fell asleep while I read. After maybe fifteen minutes an American traveler stood, walked over, and ever so gently pushed him on the shoulder. He toppled sideways onto his seat, almost in slow motion, like a lovingly felled tree. Peaceful. Graceful.

The American screamed for help, and Indonesian staff ran over and poked and prodded at the body while the Yank yelled, "Stay away from him! Don't touch him!" At the gate they announced my flight to London was delayed, "for technical reasons." I imagine finding and removing a dead passenger's suitcase from the cavernous underbelly of a 747 would be pretty technical.

However my most vivid airport memory involves another day I was trapped for hours. But that time I escaped.

I need to be busy on vacation. Lying on a beach and chillaxing drives me nuts. I have to go somewhere, see something, do stuff. I'm a pain in the arse to travel with.

In 1999 I flew to the Canary Islands, a few rocky Spanish outcrops off North West Africa, to stay at a friend's vacation place. I lasted three days. After a day exploring the nearby pretty Moorish architecture and charming fishing village, and a day driving around the island in a rented car, I was bored and ready to go home, but my return flight was four days away and my agency in Northern Ireland was closed for Easter.

So a local travel office booked me on the national airline Iberia from the Canaries to Madrid and onward to London. I would worry about the final hop to Belfast when I got there.

The flight to the Spanish capital was routine and I "de-planed" as we say today and waited for the connection. More than a decade later I still recall that despite the spring sunshine, parts of the airport seemed dark and deserted. Turned out the vast majority of Iberia staff were striking.

One after another, flights cancelled and tumbled like dominoes across the board as hoards of angry travelers descended on customer-services desks. Mine cancelled too and I was re-booked on a flight hours later. But I lurked by the desk. I knew that my new plane was never leaving the tarmac. When the last passenger had been placated and departed, I asked in pigeon Spanish, with a conspiratorial travel-professional smile, if my flight was really going. A guilty look and the minutest shake of the head later, I had my confirmation.

So hang around for hours on the slim chance I get on one of the few flights to somewhere in the UK or Ireland, or cut my losses and find a hotel? I dandered off and wandered aimlessly. Back then at many European airports sliding glass doors enclosed the international departure gates, and a hundred yards ahead passengers crowded around one.

Inside at the gate the sign read "Gatwick," London's second

airport. There was movement. Activity. Passengers boarding a bus to take them out to their plane. A flight neither posted on the departure board nor announced over the P.A.

The Spanish gate agent was shouting at the gathered Brits. "This plane full. Full. Only First Class." An Englishman yelled, "But I must get back! I must get back!" while an elderly woman shrilled, "I'll pay for First Class, I'll pay." It stopped short of pushing and shoving, but being caged for hours was fraying the nerves of even the most stoic English air-travelers.

Then the gate agent asked in Spanish, "Anyone traveling without checked luggage?" I had a suitcase in transit but I wasn't going to let that stop me. I shouted, "Si Senor!" and barged my way through the throng as he forced open the door to let me in.

You ever see that famous photograph of the last helicopter to leave the American embassy in Saigon? The soldiers are punching terrified and desperate Asians off it as it departs amidst scrambling hands and refugees clambering to get aboard. That snapshot is in my head every time I think back to this. Only with little old English ladies instead of abandoned Vietnamese.

I snatched a boarding pass reading something like Pablo Hernandez or Julio Iglesias from the Iberia employee and ran to the bus. Seconds later it sped off like a prison break.

I would be arriving too late to connect to Belfast so while boarding I called a friend in London and asked him to pick me up at Gatwick. On touchdown I even had the cheek to indignantly complain that the airline had lost my luggage. They delivered my suitcase to my home in Northern Ireland two days later.

I've been an international air traveler for more than four decades since my parents took me to Spain as a baby in 1970, so it's bizarre that this is the experience I recall so clearly. But the world changed on September 11, 2001, and I may be the last ever pasty-skinned Irishman to rush through a crowd, grab a Spaniard's travel documentation — and escape.

Hostages (October 23–24, 1975)

Alison Kinney

Extradition

Until the flight attendant delivered me into my new parents' custody, they knew me only from photographs. One head-on, one in profile, with my name printed in English on a paper tag across my chest. Baby mugshots. All the papers were in order, my arrival signed for. I was ten months old.

Freight

On my maiden voyage, I'd already flown further than my adoptive parents would fly in their lives. "She was the best baby on the plane," said the flight attendant. "She didn't make a peep." She handed me into my mother's arms and walked away.

Quiet as the kenneled pets riding in cargo. Quiet as contraband: baby birds shoved into a smuggler's pants, fruit triple-wrapped in cling wrap, bringing a taste of home and plant disease to the other place. Quiet as a stowaway, bent double and sealed into a shipping container. Quiet as a bomb, because nowadays they don't tick.

By all accounts, I made a happy American kid. Very quiet. Nobody remembers what my first word was. Sometimes the silence of our house deepened until Mom came searching for me. She'd find me under my crib or inside the closet, not making a peep.

Flight Path

We were a planeload of flight attendants and babies, who flew seven thousand miles from Seoul to Anchorage to New York City, across the International Date Line and ten time zones. I have no memory of the flight.

Thousands of other flights followed that trajectory, planeloads of babies and little kids. Some of us were old enough to remember; some have retraced our steps; some have told the rest of us what happened. What I know about it now doesn't depend on my memory at all.

Emergency Exit

Remember the last time you took a plane trip with a baby—your own, or anybody else's—the Baby On Board who presaged doom? Or the restive four-year-old, ears popping, shrieking too hard to remember to swallow?

"Are we there yet?" you cried. You considered bailing, but those were life preservers under the seats, not parachutes. Knowing there'd be no escape for the next two, ten, or twenty-two hours, you lowered your seat and ordered a drink.

Now multiply that by fifty, or a hundred. The babies, I mean. Or the drinks.

In-Flight Service

We occupied whole rows in Coach, dozens of us, apportioned five to a flight attendant. There weren't enough arms to hold us all. The flight attendants demonstrated the seatbelt and oxygen mask, waved toward the exits, served dinner—and changed diapers. They bottle-fed babies and burped them over their shoulders. They comforted, pacified, scolded, smiled and smiled, and didn't give a hoot that you wanted your drink refilled.

"She was the best baby on the plane. She didn't make a peep." Of course the flight attendant told my parents that. She'd worked a double shift on a job that wasn't her job and longed to sack out in her hotel room. She was going to say whatever it took to get rid of that baby. Nobody will sign for the worst baby on the plane.

She was the last Korean adult I'd see for sixteen years, one of only two Koreans at all. The other one was my sister, who flew to join us two years later. No, she's not genetically related to me, my sister. Or the flight attendant, either, in all likelihood.

Unclaimed Baggage

According to the adoption agency's story, I'd been three months old when I was found abandoned on the front lawn of a stranger's house.

Don't believe a word of it. Seoul is a city of asphalt and dirt, skyscrapers, tenements, and shacks. There are no houses. There are no lawns.

Many of our names were bestowed by social workers, who created legal documents and birthdays for us. They invented our status as orphans, children of the dead or of the sorrowing, hapless poor, who regretfully chose to relinquish us to better futures in America.

The agencies didn't say that "choice" was impossible, when single mothers were routinely fired from their jobs or evicted from apartments, and public assistance was virtually nonexistent. Or that agencies went door-to-door, pressuring poor parents to give up their babies. Many of us were kidnapped by aunts and uncles, grandparents, family friends, abusers, who dumped us at churches and hospitals—or, when they could find any, lawns. We vanished from short-term fosterage centers, where our parents had placed us for a couple weeks, they'd believed, just till they could land that job and reclaim us. Some of our fathers and mothers searched for years for their renamed babies, shipped to Sweden or France but labeled, in the documents, as Nederlanders or Americans.

The official story is that we were left unclaimed. Don't believe a word of it.

Some of us are stolen cargo. Captives. Abductees. Hostages.

Jetlag

I was a good flyer, but once we got "home," I started to cry. I cried all night, and the next night, and the next.

Supposedly, I'd spent my life till then in institutions swarming with children. I'd probably never been put down to sleep alone before. I didn't know this continent, this house, or these two strangers singing lullabies and rubbing my back.

I love my family. My family loves me. I'm just saying that bedtime in New Jersey was dawn in Korea, and I didn't know this time zone, either.

Airline Food

They must have distributed meals on the plane, but on the drive home, my mother fed me my first American bottle. She'd mixed my formula to half-strength. The agency had warned her that I'd be malnourished and unable to stomach regular formula.

Supposedly, I'd lived in an orphanage, then an agency-sponsored foster home, for seven months. My parents had paid the agency thousands of dollars in fees. During my babyhood, the US gave the military dictatorship in South Korea gazillions in aid and subsidies.

Somebody could have mixed some goddamn full-strength formula.

Hijackers

Piecing together other people's stories, so much gets lost, and so much becomes possible.

Halfway through that flight, perhaps everybody was dozing,

or watching the movie, on the single screen they had back then. Eating peanuts, or the real dinner you could expect even on domestic flights. Thinking, thank God those babies have piped down, maybe sparing a thought for how cute we were with our black-button eyes and onesies with nametags, napping under our baby blankets.

Until we struck.

It started with the screaming, all fifty or a hundred of us. We screamed at pitches that made eardrums bleed. We screamed the way babies scream on CIA torture tapes. We screamed to pummel you into submission, and also for the fun of it, because we'd just figured out that when we scream, you react, and that's funny.

We threw barf bags and pillows to the floor of the cabin, made you pick them up, and threw them again. Those of us whose legs were long enough kicked the seatbacks before us, right at your kidneys. "Cut that out," you said, and we projectile-vomited formula right in your eyes.

Terror in the skies!

We did not line up politely in the aisle to use the toilet. All at once, we shat ourselves, our diapers, our training pants. You reeled under the impact, but we withstood it because we were babies and we were strong and we liked to play with poop when given a chance anyway.

We took over that flight. Those of us who'd attained speech and motor skills took control and issued demands. Once we'd been hostages, but now we were saboteurs, pirates, revolution-aries.

Our demands were simple. All we asked was that you make our new home the kind of place it ought to be, where people weren't denigrated or killed for having the wrong faces. Where people weren't expected to act grateful for injustice. Where we weren't treated as special exceptions, given crumbs of privilege.

If you refused to meet our demands, we would infiltrate your families. (We are your families.) We would transform your sons and daughters into children who refused to be quiet, who yelled, protested, and tore things down. We would turn your country upside-down.

Those were our threats. For those of you who loved us, and whom we loved, these were also our gifts to you. A better world: that was all we could try to give you in return.

Stockholm Syndrome

At JFK, the flight attendants hand us over, unleashing us upon America. "The best baby. Not a peep," they say, smiling.

Separation Anxiety

Allyson Goldin Loomis

Before I get on an airplane, I prepare to die. My terror cannot be assuaged by anyone's quoting safety statistics, the laws of physics, or the training regimens of commercial-airline pilots. I cannot make myself believe that enormous buses full of people ought to climb 30,000 feet into the air. I know they do, but I don't think they should. People, born to the earth, should have the good sense to stay on it, I say—an opinion corroborated, it seems to me, by the occasional, über-deadly, airplane crash.

Still, I do fly, and with some regularity, too. I like to visit my big, nutty family in Los Angeles, half a continent away from my Wisconsin home. Plus, I enjoy seeing new places. Travel is educative, essential. I do not wish to be the sort of person who misses all the wonders of this bright planet because she's afraid to fly. I want to travel, even if it kills me, which while I am airborne, I am pretty sure it will.

On board an airplane, I am an unobtrusive phobic. If you saw me, you might note that I looked a little pale, a little sweaty. You might offer me a Saltine or an airsick bag, as a gesture of brotherly love. You wouldn't know I was having a near-death experience. In public, I try to keep it together—as might a condemned woman being carted to the gallows. I look for seat 22C. I sit. I say good-bye to the beautiful world.

Over the years I've perfected my cool charade. I am patient through long lines. I am genial to the unhelpful gate crew. No matter how strong the urge to do so, I never ask flight attendants to reassure me that the pilot is not a high-school student/drunk. Only once, during air turbulence, did I grab the hand of a stranger beside me and weep. (Only once!) But in recent years my ability to keep my head during air travel has been roundly tested.

Now, when I travel, it is always in the company of my two small children.

Traveling with small children is challenging no matter how smooth the journey, no matter how patient the crowds at security, no matter how reasonable the TSA workers, no matter how abundant and clean the bathrooms, no matter how available the bottles of milk for purchase. It is difficult even if airline personnel at the gate are helpful, even if the flight attendants are happy and well-compensated for their work and possess a scintilla of sympathy for a passenger such as I, a passenger holding a sticky eighteen-month-old in one arm and hefting a forty-pound backpack, while clutching in her free hand a fat plastic bag full of beverages and the baby's blanket, while prodding her five-year-old and his rolling travel bag down the narrow aisle, while trying to keep her own anxieties from tipping off the ragged edge of self-control.

But, generally, a parent's journey through an airport is hardscrabble, to say the least. Anyone who has ever travelled with small children will tell you similar war stories: Once I was asked to take a sip of my own pumped breast milk, to prove it wasn't Napalm; once, my child threw his pacifier into an airport toilet; once, five hours into a long delay, a man wearing a poncho advised me to discipline my kids; once, a TSA worker asked me to step into a glass box, a "holding cell." My two-year-old son, able to see me, but kept apart from me, screamed like he was on fire, and when the TSA worker tried to pick him up he vomited all over her shoes. "Oh my god," she said, "HERE," and she thrust him into the cell with me.

That's family life in the airport! Despite all these bizarre stresses, my children know me as an especially sweet, accommodating parent when we travel together. In the midst of airport hurly-burly, I croon to them: *Take your shoes off, darlings. Put your shoes on, my loves.* I let them get into and out of the stroller at will. "Watch out for people!" I call, as they caper through the wide, shining passageways. I buy them stupid snow globes, key chains, bags of Starburst, greasy "Happy Meals" — stuff I would never buy for them in our real lives. I let them climb up into the shoe-shine chairs, and I let them press their grubby noses and hands to the shining duty-free shop windows. Gently do I wipe their little fingers with the anti-bacterial Wet Ones.

I am, of course, a wreck.

"The airplane ride is going to be so much fun!" I sing, compensating for my terrible anxiety, my certainty that bringing my children on an airplane could lead to their deaths. "Do you see the big airplanes, honey?" I coo. My son runs ahead to the terminal window, his Lightning McQueen shoes flashing like mini-ambulances on the airport's corporate carpeting. A lump swells in my throat. What kind of a mother puts her children in harm's way like this? What kind of a monster am I?

These, the darkest visions of a fearful flyer, often bring me to the brink of turning back, of stuffing the boarding passes in the trash can, gathering my babies, and heading for home. I don't do it, though. I don't do it because the truth is that if I did not fly with my children, I would not be able to fly at all.

Don't speak to me of logic, of reason. Yes, I know it is crazy for a person terrified of flying to be unable to fly without her children, without putting her children at (imagined) risk. All I can say in my own defense is that I have never spoken to another mother who did not feel the same way.

"I don't mind flying," said Heather, my neighbor, "as long as the whole family is on the plane, as long as we all go down together."

"I'm so much more scared of flying now that I have kids," said my pal Kathy, "unless my kids are with me."

I asked a professional therapist about this phenomenon. He shrugged. "Some things are worse than death," he said. "Grieving a lost child is worse. That's how it seems, and maybe it's true."

"But grieving a lost parent?"

"Grieving a lost parent also seems really, really bad," he said, "especially to the parent envisioning his own loss."

No, we're not talking sense, here. We're talking about deep parent–child bonds. We're talking, I think, about love.

And so, after much wandering around the terminal with my children—after the milk, water, gum and Starburst have been purchased, after the McDonald's has been eaten, after the potty-trained have peed and the diapered have been changed—my kids and I board the plane—a plane that has as much chance of crashing as any other plane. My daughter's breath is hot on my neck. My son grips my hand taking the big step over the four-inch gap that separates the jetway from the airplane itself. Already we are too, too far above the ground.

"...As long as we all go down together."

My nerves are copper-plated. In this moment I could use a dose of peace, an unburdening of my arms. Now is the time for a brief mediation, a settling into upholstery and fate.

But my kids and I don't have seats together. Because we mostly fly Delta, the only carrier that travels non-stop from Minneapolis/St. Paul to Los Angeles, there is a 0 percent chance that my children and I have seats together, or even anywhere near each other. (I do book our tickets early. I always check in, online, twenty-four hours before take-off.) Because we fly Delta, there is also a 0 percent chance that the airline workers posted at the gate, handling standbys and strollers, will help me with my seating woes prior to boarding. There is an 80 percent chance that they will lie, telling me how they'll be happy to work on getting us seats together while the gate fills with passengers. They will smile falsely, knowing with 100 percent certainty that I will have to beg and barter for my seats all by myself.

In the airplane's foyer/galley I get right down to business with a couple of flight attendants who are greeting passengers. "Excuse me," I say, stopping traffic, "my children and I are not seated together." My voice is high and tight. I can tell by the totally lint-free dishabille of the flight attendants that they are not only childless but also petless—maybe even carpetless.

"Just take your assigned seats and we'll work it out later," says the chipper redhead, her Delta scarf pooffed and tied.

"I can't take my seats, because I can't leave my children alone." A clot of passengers is collecting behind me, pressing in.

"Just do your best," says the in-shape young man with veneered teeth.

Do my best? I wander off, adjusting my grip on the baby to accommodate for the narrowness of the aisle. Watching my son struggle with his rolling suitcase, I get a little teary, but just for a second. Pushed to this limit, my fear of flying is turning like magic—like hair turning white before the firing squad—to rage.

I choose a row in which one of the children has been assigned a seat.

Do my best? Fine.

Once, when a Florsheimed, briefcased man did not want to give up his seat, I handed him the backpack/diaper bag. "You'll find everything you need in here," I said. "If you have to change a poop, there are plastic bags and some Purel in the side pocket." I told another reluctant seat-trader that I paid babysitters $8.00/hour, that I wouldn't pay him a dime less.

"Aw geez! That's my seat," said a woman, seeing me planted in 38E with my kids at my sides.

"That's okay," I said. I'll let you have your seat." I moved to get up, and my son screamed like he did the time the TSA worker put me in the glass box. "Honey, try not to puke," I said to him, only half-kidding.

Always, during these negotiations I am breathless with disbelief at my own rudeness, my own rising ferocity. I shouldn't be surprised: If it's true that I would sooner die with my children than be separated from them, then the smaller threat—some might say the metaphorical threat—of separate seats, separate rows, separate emergency exits, triggers something uncivilized and instinctual in me.

The last time I flew, the airplane was jammed, the seating arrangements particularly tangled. A man in cargo shorts who looked like he hadn't slept in weeks, who looked like he'd been wandering airports from Jakarta to Minneapolis, displaced my daughter, sat down in our row's aisle seat—his assigned seat— and refused to move.

"I'm too tired," he said.

I installed my daughter in the center seat and stood in the aisle, staring down at Mr. Cargo-Short's ball-capped head. A few passengers squeezed past me with their duffels.

The flight attendant spoke doom into the mike: "If you don't all take your seats and stow your luggage, we won't be cleared to take off on time."

Where was I to go? My children gazed up at me, worried. "We'll be fine," I told them.

The flight attendants weren't so sure. They begged Mr. Cargo-Shorts to take a window seat two rows back.

"Only if you give me free tickets," he said.

"We don't do that anymore," said the flight attendant.

The man shrugged. The flight attendants scrambled. They managed to move a passenger, to liberate a window seat behind our row.

"You can sit with your daughter, here," the flight attendant said to me, "and your son can sit in the row behind you, just one seat behind you."

My son, only six, looked scared.

"I will not be separated from my children," I said.

"Just one seat behind you, ma'am," said the flight attendant.

"I will not be separated from my children," I repeated, this time loudly so that the passengers around me quieted down and listened. I could feel my chin quivering with nerves, but I could feel, too, the warm rightness of my position. I stood up taller.

"This plane does not fly until I am seated with both of my children."

Mr. Cargo-Shorts shook his head at me.

I picked up the baby and we stared back at him—a two-headed mommy monster. "I am not fooling around," I said.

I could see that a group of expletives were congregating behind his teeth, but he did not utter them. What stopped him? Was he a little bit afraid of me? Of me? I put my hand on my hip and raised my eyebrows, like a mother waiting for her child to shape up.

He finally gathered up his magazine and his water bottle and moved. The people sitting in surrounding rows burst into quick applause.

I did a little curtsy and took a seat.

"You did good, Mama," said my son.

"I did well," I said. I fastened our seatbelts and pulled a coloring book and crayons out of the backpack.

"I was worried," he said.

"I told you we would stick together," I said. The plane pulled slowly away from the gate. On the tarmac below a member of the ground crew swung his marshaling wands toward the west. "There's nothing to worry about, sweetheart."

For the first time in my life, I almost believed it.

Flying without Children

Sarah Allison

Today, I'm sitting in an exit row. My backpack is underneath the seat in front of me and, if I need anything, like a pencil or a hair tie or a paper to grade, I will reach down, unzip my bag, and get it. I don't have an adorable twenty-pound toddler on my lap to dimple and be squished or handed to his father. In fact, the bag is zipped, which my under-the-seat carry-on never is when I have one or both kids. Then it's an open shoulder bag containing (1) a big Ziploc full of freeze-dried yogurt bites and z-bars (I try to get through the fruit in the car or at the airport because it's so heavy), (2) water, and (3) an old Urban Outfitters bag with books and stickers and several smaller Ziplocs filled, respectively, with tiny cars, McDonald's toys, novelty dice, finger puppets, and Duplos. And, of course, (4) wipes I can reach with one hand at any time, a travel pack kept separately from the diaper kit, which goes in the big backpack stored overhead with the things that amuse me—the computer, the books, the crossword—which I will not need during flight.

In my bag right now are forty-four graded papers and eighteen ungraded papers; an article due to my colleagues for review tomorrow; some trail mix, largely chocolate; and no water, so if, for some reason, I have to dart through Denver without buying a snack, I will be hungry and thirsty by the time I get home. But I am an adult! I fast on Yom Kippur; I gave birth with no painkillers; I am bold; I travel light.

Today, I am alone and not get-at-able. I order hot drinks, carry one heavy shoulder bag instead of seven scrupulously packed ones. I look coolly on at security, confident of not raising resentment in the minds of the people behind me at the sight of all the backpacks and strollers. I smile sympathetically at people with children and shake my head as if I don't know how they do it. I sip my Coke—no discussion about what I'm drinking and who else maybe should get to have one—and assess their air-travel management practices before going back to my novel, or my grading, or a more discreet observation of my fellow passengers. I pause longest on the children, musing how their little boy's hair got past his ears without getting in his eyes. He is adorable.

For now.

My children have flown many times. Despite their practice and strong records of allowing themselves to be quietly amused or put to sleep, it would not be fair to say that they are as good as I am about sitting still for hours at a time. They are not. It is hard on them, and that's not their fault. The guy who texted "shit. baby next to me" can go to hell. I'm sure he was never a baby. As it was, he was raptured up to First Class.

Being without my children now reminds me, sweetly, of being with my children. The peculiar isolation of the row of seats, where now I don't even look at the person next to me, is then a shared isolation with my favorite young people. Only when they make too much noise or kick do they spoil the illusion that it is only us, playing together hours on end in close, hyper-focused togetherness. We cuddle, read, and play with stickers and we all know that I'm not going to get up or look at my phone or get ready to go somewhere. Instead I use all the powers of my being to keep them calm, quiet, happy. Even when they are playing more or less independently, I attend, just to keep the wheel spinning. Airplanes: never more together, never more apart.

Unlike my one- and three-year-old, I do not find it hard to amuse myself for hours on end. I am an English professor with years of yoga behind me, and I can sit still for a long, long, long time. There is work, there is sleep, there are in-flight magazines and styrofoam cups of coffee which, if you don't fly Delta, come with real cream and which, if you do fly Delta, come with those delicious cookies. I eat these now, with my coffee, instead of putting them in my bag for *later*, for the event foreseeable in its outlines but not its details: the refusal at baggage claim to get back in the stroller; or the reasonable and final-seeming refusal to get into the reinstalled car seat for the final leg home. When inconveniences beset me and my fellow travelers, I hold my comments and my pee. Whoever is going to misbehave on the plane or in line, it is not going to be me, and I know it will not be my children, either. They are home with their lovely father, engaging in the activity appointed for the hour (usually, at the times I've found myself in those lines, sleeping in their little beds). No, sir. I will stand there, with my novel or my phone and my sure sense that this, too, shall pass. My adult metabolism and practice finding the peace always there within supports me in even the longest line for a hotel voucher.

But then—a hotel voucher! That has not happened. I have not been so delayed. The sweet sense of flying unprepared, of abandoning the parent's obsessive preparation against the small hurdles of traveling, is, of course, to be understood against the terror of being apart from my children. I am far from them and out of reach. They are at the mercy of their circumstances, I of mine. We are not fighting together. I am not there to protect them or soothe them or club zombies for them. Flying as a passenger is a caricature of how little power we have to prepare for the eventualities that matter most—and flying without my children is a discipline in this truth.

Unaccompanied

Lisa Kay Adam

As our flight lifted over the city, he thought he could pick out which house was his friend's, the one with the swimming pool — among house after house with pools sprawling in the paisley pattern of subdivisions below us. Then he claimed he could make out the tracks that he and his dad had made in the nearby desert with their dirt bikes. Yeah, that was the place they had gone: "It was so cool."

Twenty minutes into his cheerful, continuous, and revealing chatter, I was not so surprised when my seatmate said, "...and that's why I'm a drug and alcohol baby."

However, I had been surprised when I had first eased myself past the man sitting in the aisle seat to get to my window seat, and he had piped up, in a breaking voice, "So where you going?" He was just a kid, an overgrown kid of twelve, I found out shortly.

He was flying unaccompanied and cross-country to see his "birth mother." He told me right off the bat. From an airline-issued plastic bag hanging around his neck, he pulled out various boarding passes and schedules to show me his destination. But the slippery pieces of paper defied easy re-insertion into the bag. I finally offered to hold his packet of gum, which he also clutched, hoping that with both hands he could get his documents straight before they slid down the aisle or under other seats.

"I've met her before," he continued, as he finished rearranging his travel documents. He casually chatted about the birth mom's various "challenges," but how she was all straightened up now, so he was going to spend a month with her this summer. Then he pulled out his smart phone and began showing me photos and videos of various car wrecks that had happened on the dangerous intersection near his home.

As our mostly one-sided conversation continued, I could see other passengers glancing our way, though whether in curiosity, irritation (they were trying to connect with their own smart phones or tablets), or sympathy for me or the boy or both, I couldn't tell. And I didn't care. I was taken by his ingenuousness.

From clues in his chatter, I could make out the benevolent influence of some adults in his life. They probably couldn't control his garrulousness and his fixations (e.g. car wrecks), and they couldn't undo some of his family history, but someone had tried to overlay these qualities with some firm precepts and manners. Without any vehemence, but as if rehearsed many times, the boy condemned driving under the influence, drugs, driving too fast, not looking carefully before crossing the street, and making fun of other children. With the flight attendants and me he always added please, thank you, no thank you, yes ma'am, no ma'am.

I could also guess from his stories what were the likely agents of his education. Teachers, of course—he mentioned that he was sad that the best teacher in the world was moving to another level and he wouldn't have her again. And family—another Mom and Dad he mentioned turned out to be his grandparents, whom he lived with now. I never understood which set of grand-parents, or whether there was a non-birth mother or stepmother, or why or when his father had died. The boy didn't hide, sugarcoat, or dramatize his reality, but it all came out in a circular fashion. His father hadn't "passed on" or "passed away." The boy just mentioned, in a casual and incidental clause in a much longer and unrelated story, "My dad's dead." Just like one of the people in the car wrecks.

I wondered if he had any worries about our own fate. In the first few minutes of the flight, he had chatted about air pressure in airplane cabins and the aerodynamics of airplane wings.

"I like science class," he added by way of explanation, but it was all theoretical knowledge and possibly a bit of bravado. With the very first change in engine noise, he abruptly stopped his own story to ask, "What's that noise? This is my first plane ride," he confessed, "so I don't know all these noises." I offered him the window seat several times, but he refused, only sometimes craning around me to look out, and quickly settling himself back.

We both worried about his connecting flight. I reassured him (without being certain myself) that the airline would have someone to take him from one gate to another, but there were other complications. He explained that this airline did not allow unaccompanied minors to travel on the last flight of the day to any particular destination, and this was his third try in a week to make the trip. Two previous flight delays had meant a missed connection, a last flight of the day, and a cancellation of his whole trip. When our flight began losing time due to thunderstorms, he confided that he didn't have any money to pay for a motel room if he couldn't make the next flight. I reassured him the airline would put him up if necessary (would they?), and that to make his connection in time, he might even get a ride in a special cart across the airport. That seemed to allay some of his worries, but there was one last problem to face.

As our flight began its long descent, he became quite flushed and sweaty. No more chatting, and no more peeking out the window around me, even though interesting ground features came into view. Finally we touched down, and he ventured two comments that displayed his touching mix of bravado and candor—"Good landing," as if he had experienced hundreds, and "I'm so glad I didn't throw up." I agreed on both counts.

The flight attendants reminded him to stay in his seat while the other passengers exited. I knew this was routine, but still it somehow felt like he was getting left behind. While filing out the aisle, I turned around to wave one more goodbye to him, and, as if he had forgotten his manners, he chirped back, "Nice meeting you!"

On another recent flight I sat next to two young brothers traveling alone. Curious, when I came home this time I did some reading on the Internet about these young voyagers. More and more minors make these solo flights; according to a 2007 *New York Times* article, "American Airlines alone flew over 200,000 in one year; Southwest, 100,000." Though generally routine, the flights pose some perils. The article recounted one mix-up where a boy had missed his connection by falling asleep in the terminal, and somehow another boy was sent in his place. And my young friend had revealed to me some of the worries and fears these children might harbor.

Why so many children flying alone? Many reasons, of course, some a factor of our relatively affluent nation. Parents can afford for their children to attend distant summer camps or visit extended relatives. But as I read on, I realized that despite all our "connectedness," there is also a whole lot of brokenness in the world, and some of this accounts for these young travelers. Marriages break up, and families break up, and every year countless adults spend money to fly their kids, solo, cross-country, to meet up with the exes, the other parents, or the birth parents.

The children who can make these flights are in some ways the fortunate ones. My seatmate revealed that his family had saved up a long time for his trip. And as I write this, I can't help but think of other families who are just now sending their unaccompanied children on even more difficult and costly trips. I live near the Mexican border, where thousands of minors have been crossing without their parents into the US. They, too, are flying—albeit on foot or in car or van—flying from danger and hunger, and looking for safety and far-away relatives. They, too, come out of a brokenness. Whole countries, and whole systems of governance and distribution, can be broken. I've realized that there are so many children, some with every advantage and some with many strikes against them, bravely traveling alone, all over the world.

The Doctor's Wife

Anya Groner

Six weeks after our wedding, my husband and I were on a plane flying back to New Orleans, where we live. We'd just reached cruising altitude and the pilot announced that we had a tailwind and might reach our destination early. Already, my husband's head tilted forward in sleep.

The previous year had been the hardest stretch of his medical training. As a resident in internal medicine, he often worked thirty-hour shifts. When rounds ended, he'd come home and dictate notes. Frequently, he had no energy left for conversation and I'd find him snoozing in an armchair with the light still on. A few hours later, he'd wake up and go back to work.

"I'm trying to survive," he told me, when I complained about his schedule or the way work consumed him. "I'm doing the best I can."

His answer troubled me. I wanted to support him as he pursued his dream of becoming a doctor, but the more time he devoted to navigating residency, the less time he had for me. I couldn't help feeling that his occupation and I were in competition. My heart hurt.

There was no turbulence when the seatbelt sign clicked on. A woman's voice came over the speakers and asked if a doctor or nurse was on board.

My husband didn't stir.

I put my hand on his shoulder. He was so chronically tired that a week earlier he'd confessed to me how much he looked forward to napping on the plane. "Sweetie," I whispered.

We were already living together when he proposed. He'd cooked a dinner of garlicky shrimp and bean cakes and asked me to fetch sauce he'd reheated from the microwave. I pressed the gray button that released the plastic door, but instead of a steaming bowl of molé, amid the splats of dried spaghetti and other brown dribbles was a navy blue box. Atop a bed of velvet was a ring.

The loudspeaker clicked again. "I repeat," the flight attendant began.

A few rows in front of us, a woman pressed her call button.

My husband's work life was a mystery to me. He'd seen me teach, but I'd never seen him practice medicine. Because of patient-privacy laws, doctors can't bring visitors on their rounds.

I knew someone else had volunteered, but I shook my husband's shoulder, anyway. "Wake up," I said. I wanted him to be the hero. "They need you."

Groggily, he raised his hand. A flight attendant inquired about his medical license and together they walked down the aisle, vanishing behind the curtains that separated First Class from the rest of us. Whatever the emergency, it wasn't in Coach.

After he left, I thought I might sleep. I tried reading. I looked out the window. For years, marriage seemed as distant and inscrutable as the green and brown patchwork below me. It was, I'd thought, the kind of tame choice that signals a loss of momentum and spontaneity. I'd felt giddy about love but ambivalent about becoming a wife. The word itself seemed like an erasure, privileging domesticity over desire, association over achievement. In marriage, I'd seen women lose their names, their ambition.

After our engagement, I asked my husband-to-be if anyone had pointed out that he was going to be a writer's husband.

"Why would they tell me something I already know?"

"I've never heard the phrase *doctor's wife* so much in my whole life."

I told him how people kept congratulating me on his profession, that a colleague said, if she were me, she'd give up teaching, that a grad-school friend asked when I'd quit work.

"Why would I do that?" I responded.

"If they're saying you're a gold digger," he pointed out, "you're not a very good one." He'd only recently divulged his med-school debt, a number he'd refused to share for years. My not-yet-husband kissed my forehead. "Who cares what people say?"

Before the plane's descent, the flight attendant returned to my seat and told me to gather my things. I envisioned my husband at the other end of the plane, performing chest compressions or birthing a baby, and followed her up the aisle. Passengers adjusted their headphones. Children wiggled in their seats. There was an emergency on board, but the crew was professional and, for most, the event didn't register. We passed through the curtains to where the seats were leather and leaned all the way back. A businessman drank a cocktail. His suit jacket hung on a velvet hanger. In another row, my husband sat beside a pale woman in a suit. Her forehead was sweaty. She sipped water and nodded while he talked.

He'd planned to propose someplace beautiful, he once told me, but then he realized he was most enthralled with our ordinary life—watching *Frontline* in bed, drinking coffee on the porch. "That's why I chose the microwave," he'd explained. "Plus, I knew you wouldn't suspect it."

The flight attendant pointed at the empty seat beside the businessman. "You've been upgraded," she said and thanked me for sharing my husband.

When the plane landed, an EMT crew escorted the sick woman to a stretcher they'd set up in the jetway. My husband recited numbers to a paramedic who wrote notes on the palm of her blue plastic glove. I waited until we got to baggage claim before I asked if the woman he'd treated would be okay.

That night, we sat together on the thin futon my husband's owned since college. His soggy medical license was drying on the coffee table; the flight attendant had accidentally set it down on the ice bin in the galley. He told me that when he saw the woman in the suit slumped against the cabin door, he assumed she was dead. "I thought there was a terrorist on board, that she'd been shot." He opened the plane's medical kit, and held a stethoscope to her chest. He had trouble hearing her heartbeat over the roar of the jets. He checked her blood pressure, and she whispered that she kept medicine in her bag. She swallowed some pills, and he sat beside her until the plane touched land.

He put his hand on my ankle. "It was barely an emergency," he said. "The seizure was over before I arrived."

I squeezed his hand, thankful to be married to a man who didn't exaggerate his self-importance. "You were there if she needed you."

"I didn't do a thing."

I felt his fingers slide down my foot, until they rested in the space between my first and second toe, where the dorsalis pedis artery passes over the cuneiform bones. Early in our relationship, I would've asked what he was doing, but by that point, this maneuver was familiar. My husband, the doctor, was checking my pulse.

Free for Flying

Nicoletta-Laura Dobrescu

In 1998, I flew for the first time when I was a second-year university student in Romania. Many people may find it rather late for a first flight, but at the time nobody around me thought so. I was one of the few lucky students in my university to get a three-month, full scholarship abroad. I was the first to fly in my family, the first in my group of friends, and a rarity for the inhabitants of my little town.

Among the graduates of my high school, I was one of the few, as well. And probably one of the even fewer to fly away convinced that I wanted to come back soon. Most of the graduates of my high school who flew before me were some of the outstanding Mathematics and Physics Olympics winners; they flew for good to America or Canada.

To many people in my community, flying meant fleeing, and the one who flew was to become for a while a little urban legend. They were not flying from one airport to another, but from a closed country to an open world. A country closed from the inside for forty-five years, and then closed from the outside in order to limit the immigration of its citizens. Nobody without a visa could get an airline ticket to the free world, and getting a visa was more difficult than getting a degree.

My access to the world "free for flying" was difficult. Being both married and a student used to raise suspicions to the foreign embassies. In my case, the suspicions and the complicated bureaucracy nearly canceled my departure. Intensive, last-minute interventions were, eventually, effective in providing me with a tourist visa, which covered most of the time I was supposed to spend abroad.

Fortunately, I arrived on a beautiful morning at the end of

August at Otopeni Airport in Bucharest, holding the "freedom and liability certificate" in my hand which read *Boarding Pass, Bucharest – Copenhagen*. I joined the queue in front of the check-in office, with my mother and my husband next to me, trying to reestablish my self-confidence. My mother was assuring me that my family would be waiting for my call, ready to send me extra money, warm clothes, food, or even another return ticket if things didn't go well; and, my husband was giving me the last instructions about the money exchange, documents safety, contacts of the Romanian Embassy, in case of problems.

Only a few steps before the office line I realized that I wasn't going to see them at all for three months, that I was stepping into the unknown, and that for the first time in my life I would be completely alone, without my family, without my teachers or friends, without anybody known, not even with my own language. Only a brief kiss and goodbye were allowed, and the queue pushed me in front of the check-in officer, then to passport control, and right towards the boarding gate.

Waiting there a while gave me the feeling that I had left my dear ones too soon, that I could have stayed a little longer, that all that blessed time with them had been lost for good. I felt wrecked in the midst of a crowd where the few Scandinavians—donning blond hair, fashionable clothes, and detached attitudes—were easy to distinguish from the recognizable Romanian majority.

I entered the airplane as I would have entered a tunnel. Compared to the brilliant August morning outside, the airplane seemed like a coffin. I didn't have to think about airplane-crash stories (although I knew a recent one, from Balotesti in 1995) to imagine my death in that airplane. I was both absorbed by this thought and extremely angered by it. The exaltation produced by the take-off and the fabulous view of the enormous green field of Baragan, bordered by the blue of Arges and Danube Rivers, made death seem so perfect from that height that wanting it became bearable, inviting, seductive.

I kept looking at the land until a thick, white quilt of clouds covered it, protecting my dear ones down there from my desperate thoughts. Noticing my recovery from my gazing through the airplane window, my neighbor asked me something, some kind of generic ice-breaking question. His deep black eyes, dark skin, and intense black hair made me doubt that the man next to me was Romanian, in spite of the perfect, elegant Romanian in which he spoke to me. We started a conversation, which revealed my neighbor to be an Iraqi, who studied architecture in Romania, married a Danish woman, and moved to Copenhagen. He kept in touch with his family in Iraq, but had never returned to his homeland after his graduation from university. He told me that he used to fly very often, for business, in different countries, as a Danish citizen.

As I had no air-travel history, I touched on the issue of the visa and confessed my anxiety about the stay in Denmark as a tourist, while in fact being a full-time student. His calm answer stood as evidence that Denmark treated the people inside its borders with a lot more confidence than the ones outside. I was to discover a little later that he was right.

I turned back to the window, to see the dark North Sea. I was absorbed into the sun's reflection on the backs of what I figured out to be a group of whales. For a while, I was tempted to look back again to my neighbor and see if there was any reflection of the Tigris and the Euphrates in his eyes, since he had first seen them from the world above. I didn't, in the end, look back at him. But I still imagine that the reflection is there.

The News from Bulgaria

Kevin Haworth

We will not cross paths with the bodies.

We are due at Ben Gurion Airport in just a few hours, and we are deep into the final busy-ness of moving out of our Tel Aviv apartment. My wife is mopping the kitchen floor, the two children are checking under the beds for any items left behind, and I am carrying the luggage down the stairs one heavy piece at a time. I return to the apartment after each trip, glad for the air conditioning, but with each piece of luggage removed the apartment becomes emptier, less *our space* as it has been for the past five weeks, and more a generic rental apartment awaiting the next customer. Soon there will be the short, hot walk to the taxi, the nighttime ride to the airport, the intricacies of Israeli security, the final spending of the shekels in our pockets on gum or chocolate, and finally, hopefully, a flight moving smoothly and relentlessly along the earth's rotation to meet the sun as it rises early Sunday morning in New York.

But one thing we know: we won't have to share the airport space with the bodies. They passed through Ben Gurion two nights earlier, on a chartered flight from Burgas, Bulgaria, one airport giving its dead to another, the sterilized transit space at either end suddenly made very personal, if only briefly, until time passes and regular flights resume.

So much of Israeli history has been written in airports. Entebbe. Vienna. Rome. Munich. In grounded hijacked airplanes and in airport lounges crackling with gunfire. In daring rescue raids made into the stuff of miracles and in botched rescues turned bloody and wrong. Even Ben Gurion, our destination tonight, is itself a part of this history, though it was called simply Lod Airport almost exactly forty years ago, when members of the

Popular Front for the Liberation of Palestine and the Japanese Red Army pulled assault rifles out of violin cases and fired indiscriminately into the crowd, murdering twenty-six people, most of them Christian tourists from Puerto Rico. Or the alternate Israeli history that could be written in flight numbers: Swissair 330, Sabena 571, TWA 480, El Al 426, El Al 253, El Al 432, like entries in a most particular and morbid travel itinerary.

Now comes Burgas, a tourist town on the Black Sea many people had never even heard of before last week, before the explosion, the bodies, the wounded. (When I mentioned the event in class, a student said, quite simply and earnestly: *Bulgaria?*) Burgas, like all the attacks before it, is now built into the Israeli encounter with airports and airplanes, an ever-evolving series of expectations and procedures, scans and questions, excitement and worry, the emotional background noise that mixes with the flight announcements, the steady drone of human conversation, the unhappy babies, the stern warning *Please do not leave your luggage unattended.*

Even in more normal circumstances, there is something about imminent travel that turns my sensible, practical, detail-oriented wife into a festering anxiety bubble. She worries. She cleans obsessively. She has terrible fantasies about burning planes and emergency water landings. She writes notes to her friends that say, regarding the children and me, *at least we'll all be killed together.* This happens every time, recent terrorist attack or no, though I know that the news from Bulgaria isn't helping. We are putting ourselves and our children into danger every time we take off and land.

Still, we go to the airport.

When we arrive, the lines are long, as they always are on a Saturday night, since Shabbat has ended and all of Israel is free to travel again. If you hadn't been reading the newspapers, or listening to the radio, or watching the television (though what Israeli hasn't been?) there would be no sign that this week was different from any other.

Soon the small, attractive Israeli security guard is holding open my passport, with its numerous entry and exit stamps for Ben Gurion-Lod, and looking at the document and at me at the same time. She asks: *Is this your first time in Israel?*

My sixth.

You don't speak any Hebrew?

I do.

Where did you learn?

Kibbutz Ramat Yochanon, near Haifa. In Ulpan.

You didn't know any before that?

I learned some, for my bar mitzvah.

Where was that?

Congregation Ezrath Israel. In New York.

Do you still go there?

I don't live there anymore.

Oh, she says. And then somewhat nonsensically, *I'm sorry.*

I've heard all these questions before, exit and entry. I answer them fully, precisely, like filling in a crossword. I've done this enough to know that the content of the questions is hardly the point. She's looking for a hesitation, an inconsistency, a nervousness—something that will make me stand out from the hundreds of people waiting behind me. She leaves with our passports in hand and gives them to another small, attractive security guard, who comes back to us. She says, *Sorry if I repeat some of the questions my colleague just asks.* Then she asks all of them, again, and we give the same answers, again.

It's all so normal. It always is. Things are normal until the terrible moment that they aren't. Even from Burgas, the eyewitness accounts reinforce the routine of air travel, how much we are able to put all this out of our minds for the nearer anxieties and bothers of long lines, luggage retrieval, bad air, bad food, boredom that feels almost sacred when set against the other possibilities. "We were just getting on the bus when suddenly someone came near the bus's front door and exploded," one Israeli tourist testified. "We heard a boom and the next thing we saw were body parts scattered on the ground...a burned hole in the side of the bus."

After the second round of questions the guard folds our passports and hands them back to us. The security officers turn their eyes to the next family. Our luggage slides through the system and receives its tags. The passengers around us board their packed, noisy flights. The wheels go up. Everyone hopes to land somewhere.

Somewhere to the West, Maybe in South Dakota

Peter Olson

We just sat there for a few seconds, peering into the snow and ice crystals dancing straight at us into the windshield, front-lit by the landing lights, total blackness beyond, shaking and rattling in the strong west wind, while the pilot held the brakes on, as much to prevent our being blown backward into a drift as to prevent our launching into the driving snow. He slowly urged the shuddering engine up to full revolutions before releasing the brakes and snapping the little single-engine plane forward into the night and the heart of the blizzard...and as he did, he let out a deep, "Hooooooooweeeeeee" of sheer delight, or terror...but there was no time to figure out which...

I don't remember anymore the urgency behind the transfer of the young cancer patient from Mackinac Island in the middle of that January night. I simply remember that the doctor at the Medical Center had been a medic in Detroit once, and we trusted him; our patient was stable, but in pain, and we all had a sense that the end was coming sooner rather than later. We also knew that neither the fixed-wing air ambulance from Traverse City nor the Coast Guard's big helicopter was willing to fly that night. Maybe the weather was just too bad, but those decision-makers had no personal connection with our patient, which was, of course, understandable. So we had called the boss of the air service in St. Ignace, and he said he'd see if his new pilot wanted to do it.

Our patient was almost exactly my age, with a daughter between mine, and a husband woven just as tightly into the fabric of the little island and their marriage as she was. Even though I had brought along extra blankets, had wrapped and tucked her into as snug a cocoon as I could, careful not to dislodge the fragile IV line snaking out to the bag I hung from a protruding fitting in the cabin, I was still worried about her not being able to move much, strapped to the uncomfortable transfer cot, itself strapped into the space we created by removing four of the six seats in the little plane. I remember that we communicated mostly by touch. I crouched beside the cot, wedging my knees and legs into the almost-space between the cot rails and the skin of the fuselage, watching bands of ice form along the ribs of the plane's structure as our breath condensed in the frigid air, before the pilot switched off the dome light and launched us into the night towards St. Ignace, in calm weather, a flight of only five or six minutes. I eased my hand through the folds of blankets, gently searching for hers, ostensibly to check her warmth, but mostly, simply to reassure her, to let her know that we would not let go of her up here in the cold. And the world compressed into our two hands, motionless, silent in the dark beneath the din of the engine and the wind. There was nothing more I could do.

Seconds later, it seemed, we bounced, then skidded on the icy surface of the runway in St. Ignace. I slid my hand from hers and began to check again the blankets, the cot straps, retrieved the IV bag from its makeshift hook and placed it gently beneath a layer of blanket under the loosened chest strap, tucking the plastic tubing carefully beside the outline of her arm, protecting it from an inadvertent snag that would undo the difficulty of getting the catheter into her veins, already brittle from the months of chemotherapy.

As we rolled toward the little terminal, still buffeted by gusts of snow, I could dimly make out the interior lights of the pre-warmed waiting ambulance as I struggled to stretch out the numbness in my cramped legs. And after the pilot had shut us down, then crawled gingerly around the head of the cot to unlatch the side door, the wind and terminal lights blasted together into the sudden opening, along with the face of the other medic who would take over her care for the ground transport to the hospital. We couldn't have known then, but this medic and I would go on to work together nearly eight years, through many nights like this, watching our kids grow up together, watching his wife battle cancer from her own angle, too. But that was years in the future, then. I remember he was all gentle business, rechecking the blankets, the cot straps, the path of the IV line, and he leaned in, through the howling wind, and said something quietly into the ear of our patient that brought a small smile to her face even as she grimaced and her hand sought mine for one last squeeze. And then they were gone. Rolling quickly through the snow, into the back of the waiting ambulance, then on into the night to the hospital forty-five ground miles and a peninsula away. I never saw her again.

And as I turned from the departing truck, I saw the pilot slowly moving to push the little plane into the protective safety of the open hangar, but as I walked over to help him push, I felt a deep, selfish stab of longing for my own wife and two daughters, back across the frozen lake, safe, I hoped, snuggled into their own blanket cocoons against the storm that was clearly intensifying. And so the words were out before I even really had time to feel ashamed, "Uh…you wouldn't want to take me back, eh?" And in his eyes, lit by the terminal arc-lights, tearing and blinking against the wind and sleet, I saw the twinned emotions of fear and delight scud quickly past before his bravado buried them with, "Aw, man…really?" But I'd seen that delight, too…

I'd met his boss fifteen years or so before, who in his turn had introduced himself to me by saying, "Hey…why don't you sit up here next to me?" before flipping his own little plane nearly onto its wingtip just after take-off simply to scare me with a joke he'd foreshadowed with a raised eyebrow to my wife, whom he had known for thirty years. After a baptism like that, I had grown used to the challenges of flying to and from the island in all kinds of weather. But my first flight with this new pilot before me earlier that year hadn't gone especially well. Coming back after a night shift at the hospital in Sault Ste. Marie, I'd wedged myself into a seat beside plumbers and masons hoping to get an early season start to the summer projects. After flying with the boss for years, this new pilot's scrupulous attention to the pre-flight safety checks struck the plumbers and me as a little too prissy. I confess that I hadn't really known some of the things about the plane I'd flown in dozens of times before until he pointed them out that morning. To make matters worse, as we spiraled up and up after takeoff, only to look down far below us to see the boss's own plane skimming along just above the waves and remaining chunks of ice, the new guy said firmly, "Nothing more useless than air above you when something goes wrong." And we all sort of bristled at the quiet insubordination, even as we uneasily knew he was right. And that unease flickered for a moment into outright panic just after touchdown on the island that morning, as the little plane skidded sideways on a patch of early morning ice…terrifying to see the runway rushing beneath me, along the same axis as the wing. But the new guy just calmly adjusted a bit, let out a quiet, "whoa," and turned us 90 degrees back to the right, back to rolling, rather than skidding sideways down the tarmac. And we were all impressed. I heard somewhere later that he had a military background, polished by seasonal crop-dusting work somewhere in South Dakota, I think.

Maybe that confidence was what allowed me to ask him to consider taking me back, knowing that it would mean not one, but two more trips out into the storm for him. I knew the outlines of another story, too, of his boss's walking bloodied into the bar in St. Ignace years before after ditching on the ice doing a patient transport on a night a lot like this one…but there was that delight thing, and the fact that just being able to touch the three girls waiting for me at home seemed more and more important.

And so we leapt up into the blackness, millions of icy white pinpricks streaming directly into our faces, mesmerizing us, daring us to try to follow the trajectory of just one of them, as we bore directly west, into the storm. I knew that the two turns would be critical: first to turn back 180 degrees to the east, then to turn 180 degrees again to line up for the approach to the runway, again heading directly into the storm. The pilot glanced over at me just once before that first turn, then fought the wheel slowly around to the left as we bucked and threatened to roll as he exposed more and more of the wing's underside to the storm. For an instant, the lights of the bridge appeared appreciably far beneath us as we finished that turn, and then I watched the airspeed jump as we began to use the storm to drive us forward towards home. The cabin grew quieter for a moment then, too, as the engine revolutions dropped a bit and some of our sound was blown into the dark ahead of us.

I don't know and didn't ask how the pilot gauged how far east we needed to fly before making the decision for the second turn; no landmarks were visible below us at all, and I knew that this was not the time he wanted to make an orienting pass over the airport before making a final approach: he wanted to get this one right with just one shot. And again, as he fought the wheel around to the left, wind bouncing us up against our harnesses as the little plane dropped and rose again in a crazy rhythm not her own, I glimpsed the runway lights far ahead of us and far below, amazingly exactly in line with our new course. And as he switched on the landing lights, it became increasingly difficult to tell the pinpricks of the runway lights from the driving snow streaming straight at us again. I kept my eyes focused tightly on what I thought were the lights, but gasped when those same lights appeared to leap upward nearly the whole height of the windshield during one of our drops in a gap in the wall of wind pushing us steadily back against the scream of the little engine. The second and third times, those light-jumps seemed much bigger as I worried more and more that we would simply not have enough air left beneath us to absorb the drop. I thought for an instant of the pilot from down below on a muggy, hazy day the summer before who had misjudged exactly this approach, gone around in the haze for a second pass, and arrowed the plane directly in to the towering white pines that separated the eastern edge of the runway from the bluff and the lake below. He and his wife and daughter had been lucky, managing to crawl from the crippled plane just before its tank exploded, sending them home with relatively minor burns to their airways and hands, but I remembered clearly the way they smelled, and the charred white pines ringing the wreckage were probably close beneath us now, buried in white.

Finally, after one more harness-straining drop, I glimpsed the runway lights beside us, and the snow streaming steadily between us and the ground as we lurched and bumped down the last few feet, then skidded past the first taxiway turn toward the tiny terminal, and eventually to a stop. I think we both breathed out slowly, but neither of us said a word. The pilot taxied quickly back toward the terminal, but stopped only long enough to reach over, unlatch my door, and bundle me out into the storm. Flushed with guilt now, I muttered my thanks as he smiled, shook his head, closed and latched the door from the inside, and taxied back to the east before turning around, holding the brakes on for a second again, revving the engine, and hurling just himself back up into the blackness streaked with white in the landing lights as he fought his way back to the west. I stood in the snow in the dark listening until I couldn't hear the engine any longer, then turned and began to walk the two miles back to my waiting family.

He made it back to St. Ignace that night, and I think he picked up the bottle of whiskey I left for him at the airport later that week, but we never shared more than a few words about that night again, though he always had a smile for me and I saw that delight in his eyes once or twice more that year, though in far less trying conditions. When I asked his boss at the beginning of the following winter, I learned he'd been killed over the summer; the boss wasn't sure, but he thought he'd snagged some power lines during a crop-dusting run, somewhere to the west, maybe in South Dakota, he thought.

Mapping Imagination

Anca L. Szilágyi

I'm a firm believer in write-what-you-desperately-want-to-know. Research, empathize, repeat. It's not impossible to write beyond your own experience or beyond your own precise demographic. But it is a risk. I felt daunted by the prospect of setting my first novel against the backdrop of Argentina's Dirty War, having no immediate experience with it, no direct connection to the country, yet I felt compelled to continue with the project, because I thought the period important—one that should never be forgotten. I spent years just doing research and thinking about the story that was unfolding—painfully, slowly, but still unfolding—in my imagination.

In early 2010, one of my teachers, Jonathan Raban, asked with exasperation, "Why don't you just *go* there?" It's not that I hadn't thought about that. It just seemed out of reach, too expensive. But his question lodged in my ear. Soon enough, I found two cheap tickets on Mexicana. So, in August 2010, my husband and I flew: Seattle–Chicago–Mexico City–Buenos Aires.

The Mexico City airport, a limbo place, eerily manifested previous anxiety dreams, where rooms behind rooms unsettled: one wing, where we arrived, a shopping arcade of shiny marble surfaces and sparkly merchandise, and another wing, where we departed, plagued with leaky ceilings, dim lighting, moldy carpeting. Something fancy hiding something rotten. (I had a similar experience in Las Vegas: one hotel room of glitz and rot.)

To our surprise, and delight, the flight from Mexico to Buenos Aires was half empty. We could stretch out in our row, or take up two rows, if we wished. We could wander from aisle to aisle, taking in views from both sides of the plane.

Night hid the landscape for half the trip. Only an occasional spangle of light suggested a small South American city. When a red glow slashed the horizon, we tiptoed from one side of the cabin to the other and could make out a brown, craggy desert with mountains of rock whose edges were softened, I suppose, by wind. It wasn't a landscape I'd imagined when thinking about South America. Was it the Atacama, driest place on Earth? I'd only thought of rain forest, grassland, peat bog.

We went to the Plaza de Mayo a few times. There, the Mothers of the Disappeared marched before the Casa Rosada, as they'd been doing weekly since 1977. Across the Plaza, protesters set off firecrackers or flare guns periodically, and the pigeons, periodically, flew up in terror. But life apparently continued as normal. Only we and the pigeons were visibly shaken.

Two weeks into wandering the city, talking to people who'd lived through that time (1976–1983), and leafing through stacks of old magazines at the Museum of the City of Buenos Aires, I started a complete rewrite of my novel.

A few days before our scheduled departure, we learned that Mexicana had filed for bankruptcy and cancelled all flights. In a frantic search for the Mexicana offices (no longer downtown), we took a cab all the way back to Ezeiza International Airport. It took a while to find anyone who knew where to send us—the first man at the information desk shrugged and said they simply didn't exist anymore—but at an unmarked door behind an unmarked ticket counter, Mexicana employees worked, and there, after much trepidation, we were given vouchers for a flight on American Airlines (which, ironically, filed for bankruptcy in 2011). This flight, packed to the gills and stopping in Miami, was where I stewed on all the sensory, emotional, and historical detail accumulated, and where I hoped I could finally follow Jonathan's other advice, which was, "just trust yourself and write."

In my novel, there are several attempts at flight: flights of the imagination, literal flight, and involuntary flight. Involuntary flight compelled the other forms. One horrific method of assassination undertaken by the Argentine military dictatorship, by the Navy in particular, was to drug prisoners (the "disappeared"), take them in planes over the Rio de la Plata or the Atlantic, and fling them, naked, hands tied with wire, into the water. This happens to a character in my novel.

The use of planes to terrify claimed a terrible hold on my imagination. It's not "just" 9/11, though that was certainly a huge presence in my consciousness when the novel germinated. A tension between imprisonment and flight wrenched the gut. In the third draft of my novel, I began to draw on the emotional valences of family stories of my grandfather's imprisonment (in 1940s Romania, not 1970s Argentina) and of his older brother's assassination (thrown off a train, not a plane), and I realized that what matters most, for me, much more than autobiographical tidbits, is expanding the human capacity to empathize.

Why don't you just *go* there? Jonathan had asked of the literal place. But there was also a figurative place I needed to go to that, draft after draft, I could only just burrow into a little more. The mind of the person in flight, or fall, rather: horrible freefall. I was scared. My thesis adviser, David Bosworth, had, in what seemed to be a throwaway comment at my oral defense, suggested I end the book in the perspective of the "disappeared" character—give him his due. After waving away this possibility, I decided that it was exactly right, that the most immediate way as well the most harrowing way was also the best way: to enter his mind in those last moments. What would *I* think, what would I feel, if I were him, in his situation, in those last moments—if I were in his place, if my heart thumped as his, if my thoughts raced as his, shocked from the slow stickiness of sedatives, bones shaking, what would I experience, hurtling off the plane, in freefall?

Some Say the World Will End in Fire (I Imagine Him Laughing)

Hugo Reinert

For hours, it seemed, I stood out there on the runway with the other passengers—watching the fire crews, wondering if I might still make it home in time for the funeral.

She was a cute kid, I always liked her. At gatherings back on the island she'd watch me from the corner: two dark little eyes, at table height, following me across the room. Precocious, with a hint of the unworldly, maybe ten years younger than me—small enough, for a few years, that she could pounce and wrestle me with innocence. From the day she discovered this, I had nowhere to hide, no sofa was safe. Then, one day, she was a teenager: awkwardly, the pouncing stopped.

She became the sort of adolescent whose mother would disclose, quite matter of fact, that her daughter could bend metal spoons with the power of her mind. Standing next to her, the daughter would kick her feet, embarrassed—abashed, to have her talents and accomplishments sung in public, but she never denied bending the spoons. For this, of course, I liked her all the more.

Her death was sudden, unexpected. Sleepover at her boyfriend's place, an unguarded fire that spread the kitchen. They both died in their sleep—peacefully, it was said. When the call came I was living overseas, working as a copywriter. Within two days I was on a plane, heading home.

Then, rolling down the runway, the left engine burst into flame.

The air crew, bless their souls: barely out of their teens, girls off to see the world in cheap blue uniforms paid for from their own wages. Ill-equipped to deal with the prospect of 50,000 liters of burning oil engulfing their human cargo. Struggling to contain their own rising panic, never mind ours, they shuffled down the aisle waving their hands: "Evacuate! Evacuate! The plane is on fire!" Disregarding all instructions, I grabbed my laptop—a sturdy 90Mhz of gray brick, no CD drive but it had a floppy, that is how long ago this happened—and headed "for the nearest exit." At the cabin door I hesitated. Boots on, boots off? Never mind, I jumped. And landed, sliding down that yellow chute.

Standing on the runway, watching the fire crews, I felt eerily dislocated. What if I had died on that plane, consumed in a fireball, on my way to the funeral of a girl who had burned alive? Some say the restless dead bring others into the mode of their own death: eaten by a jaguar, you become the jaguar that hunts your family. She did bend spoons, after all. Shaken, I called up my mother to let them know I'd be late. Soon enough we were escorted back into the terminal.

In *The Psychoanalysis of Fire* (1938), Bachelard tells us fire is the most intimate of elements. It takes hold and enraptures, demanding "malign vigilance" of its observer. It smolders in the soul, Bachelard says.

The aftermath was awful. Her mother never fully recovered: too often, in years to come, her face would cave in like a black hole, hollowed by sudden grief. The grave was tended with desperation. Walking past the graveyard, you'd see the flash of color among the gray stones. Favorite toys, lined up one after the other, guarding the tombstone: a pony, some dolls, stuffed animals. Later, with the rain and shifting seasons, the stuffed ones began to fall apart. The plastic ones, I think, are still there.

This happened at the tail end of the bright northern summer, when the air turns cold and crisp and the world grows vast around you but the sun still warms your skin, from far away. A day like any other, in late August 2001. Not two weeks later, the Twin Towers fell. Fireballs of airplane fuel; human smoke rolled across Manhattan and a hundred-million television screens, the world changed. Wars were launched that still run red today.

The Aztec god of fire has two faces: an old man, wrinkled with time, and a fiery young warrior, fed by the blood of lizards and the young. Huehuetotl and Xiuhtecuhtli, the double god: ember and flame, lord of warriors and of new life, renewed through the sacrifice of blood.

I still fly. Yes, I did slide down one of those yellow rubber slides, and I have yet to meet anyone else who has. But this happened in another country, strange and far away—a country of the ancestors. In hindsight, like many of the things that happened back then, she seems unreal. The film of an apparition: crepuscular mist, dispelled by the fiery dawn. I resort to guesswork. I remember those tickling fights, laced with nascent...Of course there was something smoldering there, in the play-fights. Any excuse to wrestle that older boy. You see, back then we didn't have to take our shoes off. We were allowed to travel with liquids. Laptops stayed in their bags. None of these forms that have crystallized around us, taking shape to prevent things that already happened, doors closed after bolting horses. Is it tamed? It smolders in our petrol tanks, and smoke darkens the skies.

Passing through security, every time, I sense the vastness that enfolds me: the unthinkable worldwide machinery of wells, factories, governments, mines, flight schools, supply chains, catering operators and architects, glass and steel and concrete, plastic trays and microwaves, pilots and guards and scientists and building crews and border controls and traffic controllers and legislators and security guards and air hostesses and baggage handlers, chain upon chain, layer on layer—meshed together in a world system of human labor that converges, time after time, to produce that perfect instant where I surrender myself into the hands of strangers and pass through, get a coffee, sit down at the gate with a book.

To sense its scope is to see it exposed, fragile and contingent, spider-work of a thousand delicate links—and to smell, at the heart of it, the burning oil: precious, finite, dwindling in a million engines. Sitting there, I wonder what ancient Huehuetotl would make of it all, sat under his incense bowl, presiding over the flame. I imagine him laughing, gaunt and old, face lit red by the flickering embers. Then I turn off my iPad, buckle my belt, watch the videos. Offer polite but nominal attention to the stewardesses, in their blue uniforms, and brace myself for the ascent—cloud-bound, in a tinfoil hull. How long can all this last? Somewhere, at the back of my mind, a small troupe of stuffed animals holds vigil on an island graveyard, growing moldy in the rain—decomposing toys, guardsmen, mourning a world that was cut short by fire.

The Saturated Shirt

Laura Cayouette

Almost all my favorite flying stories involve the people I've met but as I reviewed them, I realized what a name-dropper fest it all was due in large part to my many First Class flights. A young and very sweet Notorious B.I.G. was probably my favorite person to share an armrest with. It was around twenty years ago (before he'd hit the mainstream), but as a former nightclub DJ I knew just who he was. The details have faded but the feeling I got around him is unforgettable. Though it's a back-handed compliment at best, I remember thinking that he wasn't even a little attractive to me when I sat down and looked into his big, droopy eyes—but by the end of the flight, I felt all soft-hearted toward him and totally understood he had a way with women.

On another flight about twenty years ago, I was traveling with Richard Dreyfuss and two of his small children, Ben and Emily (who've both grown up to be luminaries themselves) to meet the Pope. (I warned you there'd be name-dropping). Traveling with children can be dicey and there can be a lower tolerance for youthful tomfoolery in First Class as most of the travelers in that section are usually working or resting before arriving to work.

The kids finally settled in and I tried to catch a quick nap, leaning my head against the window. Awhile later, I awoke feeling a droplet hitting my head. I tried to drift off again, but then… another droplet. I touched my head and found it wet. The liquid on my fingers was a clear, dark brown. I looked down and my shirt was saturated with coffee.

The flight attendants couldn't have been more helpful or more mortified. We figured out a line running to the Business Class upstairs had sprung a leak and they became mop-wielding MacGyvers, fixing the coffee line and cleaning everything up. We used wet towels and one of those cockamamie airplane sinks to clean my hair. But the best part was how they handled the saturated shirt-situation.

I took off my coffee-drenched top and got to put on...a flight-attendant uniform top! Like lots of women my age and older, when I was a kid "stewardesses" had the most glamorous jobs with the coolest uniforms. So, like lots of little girls, I had wanted to wear one of those cool uniforms with the fancy hairdos and too-thick makeup while getting paid to travel to exotic locales. Back in the day, the uniforms ranged from Bond girl to Jackie Kennedy-inspired. Modern ones are far more practical and less concerned with seduction but I felt adorable with those crisply-creased short sleeves and strategically-placed pleated pockets. As we flew to Rome, the flight attendants washed and dried (mostly) my shirt over the remaining hours and I left the flight like new, if a bit damp.

In 2001, I got to play a flight attendant in an American Airlines commercial. My uniform was a navy business suit designed to engender trust and convey authority. It was miles from the Mod color-blocked mini-dresses and belted shirt-dresses of my childhood fantasies—or that top I wore on my way to Rome. Advertising more legroom, the commercial was probably the most popular spot of the sixty-some that I've done. In it, I ask a passenger if there's anything else I can get him and he jokes, "I could use a little more leg room." *Vroom vroom.* I whip out a drill and get to work. After pushing his chair back and smiling, another customer raises his hand, "Oh miss...." The drill was what sold the spot, but it was also what killed it. On 9/11, American Airlines suffered the worst day of its company's history when terrorists used their planes as weapons. Suddenly, it was not cute to whip out a hand tool on a plane. The spot was yanked that day.

But what strikes me about these two uniformed events is what underlies them: life is almost invariably more amazing than acting-out-life. And so I'll always remember best my first time in uniform.

House Beautiful

Pia Z. Ehrhardt

When my grandfather died in 1985 my first husband didn't go with me to the funeral. He was out of work again. "I need to keep the job hunt alive," he said.

The call came in the middle of the night from my father. I lived in New Orleans and my parents were a hundred miles away in Mississippi, but we booked the same flight and rendezvoused at my airport. I couldn't remember the last time I'd flown with them. We'd lived in three countries but my parents loved eternally long drives. When we did take a plane my sister and I sat in the row behind them.

My marriage was in its final month, and my parents' marriage was in its final ten years. My father had taken up with his graduate student and my mother wasn't budging. I had fallen in love with someone else, too.

On this flight we sat three across with me between them, because I thought buffering was my job. In high school, I'd stay behind at the dinner table with my raving sober father; and later, I'd find my drunk mother out on the patio, and smoke a cigarette with her, drink more wine.

But on the airplane my parents treated each other with kindness, like handsome strangers who had in common the fresh loss of a parent. My father sat, sad and quiet, with a bloody Mary; my mother sipped ginger ale and thumbed through a *House Beautiful*.

The air at 30,000 feet was smooth and rare. For the first time in a long time, the discomfort of being their daughter went away. Even if we'd hit unexpected turbulence, I wouldn't have been afraid.

In the open casket, my grandfather looked dapper in a dark

suit, a starched white shirt and his favorite red tie. My mother patted his chest and kissed his forehead. "I love you, Daddy," she said. My father touched his father's cheek with the tips of his fingers and choked back a sob. I knelt and in my silent prayer I apologized to my grandfather for loving him less than I loved my grandmother.

Relatives came by the house, bringing lasagna, veal bones in red gravy, crispy fried artichoke hearts, rum cake, biscotti studded with pine nuts, and liters of red wine. People said nice things. My husband didn't phone to extend his condolences, and the family noticed. It made our divorce easier to explain.

The next day my grandmother wanted my grandfather's things gone. My mother bagged clothes and shoes and golf clubs for Goodwill, and my father brought the bags down to the rental car. My parents worked in tandem. My sister was living in Berlin and we shipped her a slouchy blue alpaca cardigan with tortoise buttons, like something Bing Crosby would wear. My father kept a signed baseball from my grandfather's minor-league baseball days. My grandmother let my mother bring home a stern, sepia photograph from their wedding day in 1929. I packed my grand-father's paisley bathrobe in my suitcase. He was a small man and it fit me.

On the plane home, my father sat across the aisle. Over Atlanta we encountered a few bumps. "Think of them as potholes in the road," I said to my mother, but she kept her warm, dry hand on my arm. I didn't want to land.

The Less-Than-Perfect Flight

Hal Sirowitz

I was on a flight from New York to Pittsburgh. All of a sudden the pilot got on the loudspeaker telling us that we're going to make an emergency landing in Harrisburg, Pennslyvania. He wasn't sure of the nature of the problem, so he didn't want to speculate. The plane seemed too heavy. They'd dropped some tanks to make the plane lighter, but he still couldn't say with certainty what was wrong.

I imagined the pilot throwing our luggage out next. I went through a mental checklist, trying to remember if I packed anything valuable. I should have taken my old toothbrush instead of a new one. Then I worried about the question of liability. With my luck my suitcase would be the one to hit and kill someone. How could I deny my responsibility? I over-packed—making it a heavier deadlier weapon. Unless from the height we were at my suitcase would burn up like a meteor and hit the earth the size of a pebble. I kept thinking of the song, "Catch a falling star and put it in your pocket." Maybe the person about to get hit by my suitcase might see it at the last second and catch it. There was always hope, though it was getting slimmer.

Then the pilot got on the speakers again to tell us that we might hear sirens and see ambulances and security cars heading for our plane, but we shouldn't worry, because it was only a precaution. He doubted whether we would need any help.

We landed in Harrisburg, only to be told nothing was wrong. The pilot made a personal appearance emerging from the cockpit to tell us that he could understand why we were mad at him for interrupting our flight but it was better to be safe than sorry. In fact, whether we want to admit it or not, there could have been something wrong with the plane. Therefore, in a less-than-perfect world his preemptive actions could have saved our lives. In fact, it only caused more delay. But he wasn't responsible for the world, only the plane. In answer to the inquiry about whether any luggage was thrown out the chute, the answer was no.

We got to Pittsburgh safe but late. I stayed in a section called Squirrel Hill. I never saw one squirrel. But if truth be told, I wasn't looking. I avoided looking up in the trees.

Airport-Only States

Dustin Michael

I.

There's a minor interrogation going on in the front of the plane. The old guy in 1C is laying it on the flight attendant, a tall redhead in her early twenties with a weary ponytail that looks like it got hassled going through security. No jewelry. No makeup. Smile that takes a couple tries, like a bent motel-room key.

Despite her nametag, I'm going to refer to her as Allie, because her widow's peak gives her ghostly pale face the heart shape of a barn owl.

Allie answers: she's had this gig five years. (There's a long layover between "five" and "years.") Says she lives in Charlotte, has ever since she started with the airline after high school. No, she doesn't want to do this forever; thought it would be fun; wanted to travel. Now they've got her pulling two to eight flights a day—four to sixteen ups and downs. Each morning, she wakes in a hotel by an airport, but can barely remember what city she's in. Can't quit right now, what with the economy how it is...

All of this is perfunctory, from the flight-safety instructions she performed, to her full-cabin choreography routine, hoisting carry-ons, tallying passengers, punctuating it with a quick return and downward spin in the galley, lowering herself onto her pop-out chair and belting in, conveniently across from the lunging, sport-coat-wearing jackal in 1C.

Trickles of light splash across Allie's porcelain features. Does she ever get sunlight that isn't torn to shreds by spinning propellers and spit through the Plexiglas of tiny ovular windows? The turboprops' howl drowns out the inquisition, but her strigine face says it all, concealing joy as efficiently as the panels hiding the aircraft's oxygen masks. As soon as we're airborne she's up, wiping the tops of cans in the drink cart, wiping the stainless-steel surfaces in the galley, wiping the sticky marks from the rubber mat.

Our flight is Hilton Head-bound. My wife and newborn daughter are there, home. We will land at the airport where I work, marshaling these small express flights, loading their cargo bins with expensive suitcases and golf bags. Forty-eight minutes estimated flight time. Ten miles visibility.

Allie passes through the cabin with a selection of beverages. I ask for a cranapple juice. She pours one, glances conspiratorially around, slides the can onto my tray. A gesture of industry solidarity?

No. She shoots me the look a woman uses to let a man know she's seen him watching her; her gaze falls to my wedding band, then rises icily back up, either at me, or, through me, to the lever on the emergency-exit hatch. It all comes through loud and clear as, "Just drink your juice, don't hit on me, and we'll all make it out of this."

I have no intention of hitting on her. It sounds as though we both took the airline job for the same reason—travel—but it's ending for me soon, and I'm not sure how I feel about that yet.

I don't say this. I drink my juice.

II.

One thing I can't prove but strongly suspect: flight attendants are some of the US's most malnourished workers. Commercial air-travel obliterates distance; the aluminum alloy fist of the passenger aircraft gathers and bunches the fabric of place, or at least of airports, chain hotels, restaurants—if those things can be called "places." For a flight attendant like Allie, who is always stuck in the boondocks without a car, a grocery store or a stove, it might as well be some isolated polar station. What kinds of forage does she find in those vast airport-exit food deserts? How often is the ring of her dinner bell sounded by the clank of coins falling into an airport vending machine?

Allie rips open a pack of peanut M&Ms, devours them one at a time.

I swivel to the window, watching the messy sprawl that's strewn over the Piedmont plateau around Charlotte appear to tug itself apart. The term for this is parallax, a trick of perception. The closer the object, the faster it seems to pass, just like the scene below: the fast foreground of roads and roofs racing at the shuffling feet of cul-de-sacs and duplexes while high-rise apartments and skyscrapers stand guard in the distance. I blink, adjust my sight, imagine the plane sits stationary, mounted on a post, the world sliding past on a conveyor belt. I could do this back and forth the whole flight.

This free trip will be one of my last. The airline is cutting back: last hired, first fired. Flight attendants have had it worse, a series of similar cataclysmic extinctions having wiped out all but the most hard-scaled flying reptiles, who folded their leathery wings tight against their Nixon-era hire dates and watched with cold yellow eyes as corporate rats picked the bones of the young. How Allie survived is a mystery. She is a creature out of place and time.

On a cocktail napkin I do a quick tally of all the states I visited on the airline's dime. I cross out the airport-only states. The captain instructs Allie to prepare the cabin for arrival.

Arrival. My wife and baby in the terminal, my own bed tonight. Allie travels everywhere. Does she ever arrive?

The last time I see her, she's ushering stragglers down the stairs. When the last passenger steps onto the ramp, Allie lowers her owl face and slouches forward between the handrails for a moment, then tosses her hair back, ducks into the cabin, and disappears.

She will keep her airline job after I lose mine, but at what cost? She's receding from the world, this woman. Or the world is receding from her. From this distance, it's hard to tell which is moving away faster, or if I'm the one moving.

It All Happened With Courtesy

Jess Stoner

It was 2000, and I had arrived at Reagan National Airport with enough time to have a beer before my flight.

It was only a few months after the Music City Miracle had yet again stuffed the hearts of every Buffalo Bill's fan into the garbage disposal, where there was already a spoon, and flipped the switch. It was the fourth quarter of the Wildcard Game, and the Tennessee Titan's Lorenzo Neal handed the ball off to Frank Wycheck, who tossed a (it wasn't *a*) lateral to Kevin Dyson, who ran down the sidelines for the game-winning seventy-five-yard touchdown. I had watched the loss alone, living in Washington D.C., far away from the lake effects and lip-chapping winds of Western New York, my home.

I piqued two business travelers' attention when I asked the bartender if she had Labatt Blue. Or maybe it was the denim skirt, the thickly knitted turtle-necked tank top, or that I finished my first beer in less than five minutes. Whatever it was, we got to commiserating and they got to buying me more. Five beers and thirty minutes later, I heard the last call for my flight.

There wasn't enough time to find the ladies room. The flight was only forty-five minutes long. And anyway, there would be a bathroom on the plane.

It was on takeoff that I realized my mistake. It was a small plane; there were less than fifty seats available and each passenger had their own row. The flight attendant, who seemed personally offended there weren't more of us, told us where the emergency exits were and that the "Fasten Seatbelts" light would never go off. I looked to the back: there was no sign that the bathroom wasn't occupied. There was no sign of a bathroom, period.

I began to pray for prevailing winds. Or whatever winds make you arrive more quickly at your destination. Twenty-five minutes into the flight, I stared out into the clouds, willing the announcement of the initial descent, and began to cry. I remembered a scene from *The Simpsons*, when Grampa Simpson held it in too long and his kidneys burst. The pain. I remember the pain. A part *down there*, near a part that I liked and wished no harm to, was about to burst. My swollen, ripe bladder pushed muffinly against the waist of my skirt.

And I thought: *I'll just pee a little bit. No one will know. It'll relieve the pressure and*—I shifted uncomfortably and promised myself I would prove false the long-proven fact that you cannot just pee a little bit.

The few seconds I let it loose were nearly orgasmic—my eyes drooped sensually, my shoulders relaxed. Until I closed the dam and felt the warm. And the pain began again, though this time worse: if registered in decibels, it would've resulted in the death of hearing tissue. I practiced square breathing through the tears. Focused on the tray table in front of me. And realized what I would have to do.

I quickly asked for another Diet Coke before the flight attendant strapped herself in for landing. And I peed myself. Time seemed to dilate. I gloriously, gloriously pissed myself, the urine pooling between my thighs, breaking the barrier of the denim and seeping into the seat. When it finished, my mind clear and my bladder empty, I knew what needed to happen next.

I moved the arm rest, scooted over to the middle seat, and poured my entire drink on that place I had ruined. And then, a different kind of miracle happened: I found scented hand-sanitizer in my backpack, squirted it on top of the wet to cut the smell, and prepared for landing.

I exited the plane and said nothing. I had wiped down my legs with notebook paper. I would not draw attention to myself.

And then I proceeded to the bathroom, where I put my ass in

front of the hand dryer and waited for my boyfriend to pick me up.

When Gérard Depardieu pissed himself before his plane had reached cruising altitude, he gave a warning to his fellow passengers, "Je veux pisser, je veux pisser." A witness explained what happened next: "...and then he did it on the floor. No one said anything. It all happened with courtesy."

And though Depardieu and I took different approaches, he didn't piss himself so much as asked if he could go, was refused, and then pulled his junk out and let loose in the aisle. I feel we are forever bonded. A kindly father, an unlikely hero.

Layover in Dubai

Thomas Beller

Airports get more scrutiny than they deserve. It's a function of
our natural panic and excitement about leaving home. The trip
has begun, and we are turned on, recording everything, eagerly
seeing, imbibing, interpreting. But what do we see? We are in a
holding area, a little ecological unit with a rapidly shifting
community that, like the people massed at a particular gate all
going to the same place, briefly have a coherent identity. Mostly,
airports assault you with an enormity that deadens you. I
sometimes think of a line from a play, I believe it was "Art," in
which one of the characters, speaking of Heathrow Airport,
blurts out in horror, "That carpet!" The one exception to this rule,
the rule that one should keep one's watchful energy in reserve for
the moment of arrival, as opposed to the airport, is the layover.
The layover can be interesting. You never set foot in the transi-
tional country in which you have landed, and yet you get
something out of the experience. You see the landscape from
above when flying in and flying out, which is no small thing. You
get some local color.

I recall spending a couple of hours in Seoul in 2011. In a local
English-language paper I read of the government's plans to invest
in K-Pop. The idea was that cultural exports could be hugely
profitable. I remember doubting this. Maybe it would get Korean
culture, in the K-pop form, wider exposure. But I couldn't
imagine the business angle. Nevertheless the overall sleekness of
the airport, the skyline, the airplane itself, which was then a
brand new enormity with sleek lounges in the back and Business
Class seats and was basically a cruise ship in the air minus the
pool, and that article all stayed with me. I thought of it a couple
of years later when my kids asked me for the thousandth time to

play "Gangnam Style." Then there was Dusseldorf—I had a great layover in Dusseldorf in 2009. In certain sleek, anodyne, orderly environments that are tinged with style, I often now remark, "This is like the Dusseldorf airport." When I went through it in the summer of 2015, I actually looked forward to that hour and a half.

Sometimes what the layover gives you is a glimpse of yourself. And sometimes, it gives you a kind of organizing metaphor for what is to come. You may not grasp this until long after the fact, but suddenly it is there.

Long before Dusseldorf and Seoul, there was, for me, a seminal layover in Dubai. A long one. I was on my way to Phnom Penh in 1994 to work for *The Cambodia Daily*, an English-language newspaper that had existed for only a year. My friend Sam convinced me to go. He would be there, too. That was the pitch. Escape, adventure, a hint of the good deed. But mostly, buddyship. Buddyship with Sam had a strong appeal. I liked being around Sam.

But I was reluctant. In 1994 the Khmer Rouge controlled the northern part of Cambodia. There was a low-grade war going on. That makes it sound as if the country had a virus, which is not an altogether inappropriate image; contagion was a metaphor for the whole region. It had once been the spread of communism that was feared. Then it was the spread of the Vietnam War. Now there was something else, a kind of wild west of money, the early tremors of globalism and its decadences and discontents. In 1994 the whole region felt like a frontier and it attracted frontier types.

Sam was this sort of person, but more perverse. An explorer, a journalist, a writer, a self-annihilator, someone attracted to precipitous moments. I loved him. Wanted to be with him. He frightened me. I knew him very well. But I had only met him a couple of years earlier. When he told me about the daily newspaper he had come across in Phnom Penh, and suggested that we fly out and write for it together, I thought he was crazy.

I turned him down. A few moments later: yes, yes, I would go, I would meet him Phnom Penh and write for the paper, at least for a while: he got out a map, unfurled it on the floor. We knelt beside it. It was an old hand-painted map on canvas. He had acquired it in Saigon the previous summer.

Five years later Sam would die, or kill himself, or misjudge, or relapse. I tire of distinguishing. I put these words down with the deadened humility and sorrow that comes with having touched on these matters in various degrees of detail in various drafts of various books. In some instances they weren't published, in others they weren't even shown to anyone. It happens. The distance of time does grant certain gifts, which brings me back to my layover in Dubai.

In Dubai I wandered in the airport for a while, my feet sliding along the extremely well-polished marble floors like some mental patient. Eventually I found my way to a bar. It was dim, mostly empty, and a large-screen TV was on. This was before they were common. It's enormity was space-age, suggestive of the wealth of the Arab world in which I had unexpectedly found myself for a few hours. A match at Wimbledon was being broadcast on the huge TV. I stared at the screen, the men in white shorts, bathed in the sunshine of a city I had just left. I took a seat. I was alone in there except for two men huddled at a table over beers. Westerners. I sat down at a table, got a drink, and watched the screen. In the middle of a long rally, the screen flickered. It was briefly covered in a film of static. The picture vanished. Then it came back. For a while the picture went in and out like this.

"Why?" I said out loud, in a mode of complaint to no one in particular. I thought it was the big freaky screen, wobbling like a giant bubble.

"The signal comes from Abu Dhabi," one of the nearby men said. Australian, his accent sharp, proficient. "There must be some weather on the Gulf."

I nodded and looked back at the big screen. Tennis players.

Men on the baseline, hitting. Now one of them is getting ready to serve. The other crouched, ready to return, rocking from side to side, squinting in the sun. Then static, a flicker, and the blackness of the dead screen. A moment later it spasmed to life. In and out. At the time this partial reception made me feel far from anywhere he had ever been.

Over the years I have thought about that dim, modern bar, that little oasis of the familiar, amidst the intensely unfamiliar sleekness of an airport populated mostly by Arab men in white, drifting around in sandals amid duty-free shops. The image of the flickering screen, Wimbledon, England, civilization, had always seemed like the center of that moment's irony. But now I feel this image of a tennis match on a screen that fades to static and then comes back and then fades again is a good metaphor for my relationship with Sam over those next five years—each disappearance or secession increasing the wish for the image to return, back and forth until the screen goes black once and for all.

Nostalgia for the Small Airport

Anna Leahy & Douglas R. Dechow

For several years, we lived in Galesburg, Illinois, a town with a small airport, a place we'd swing by, trying to catch sight of a takeoff or landing. Once, we saw a shiny silver Lockheed Constellation—a Connie—an aircraft from the 1940s and 1950s with four propellers and a triple-finned tail. Depending on who's counting and when, as many as three or as few as one Constellation remains airworthy in the United States. This Connie sat in the middle of a place many East and West Coasters consider flyover territory, gleaming in the Midwestern sunshine.

Galesburg's airport, coded KGBG, has one runway with a length of 5791 feet, another running 3600 feet, a defunct terminal building, some hangars for small planes, and a building housing a few flight-related businesses. It has no control tower, though it turns the lights on from dusk to dawn and even the wind indicator is lit at night. Though it was once served by Ozark and Britt airlines, it's easy to think nothing happens at KGBG anymore. Still, in 2010, it served as home to more than thirty aircraft and averaged thirty-eight operations a day.

Every year for four decades, on Labor Day, dozens of Boeing Stearman planes descend on Galesburg for an annual fly-in. For 2011, that meant 137 of the 1930s- and 1940s-era biplanes from thirty states. Most are painted the Navy's yellow or the Army's blue and yellow because the aircraft was originally a military trainer, but some are black or red. Former president George H.W. Bush and former astronaut John Glenn trained in Strearmans. In fact, the youngest pilot at the 2011 fly-in arrived in the 1942 aircraft Bush had flown during World War II. When we lived in Galesburg, we stopped by to walk amidst the beautifully restored aircraft, talk with pilots, and shade our eyes to watch fly-bys, formations, and tricks in the sky. In these moments, time slows for us, and we catch our breaths together. The fly-in lasts a week, with a fly-out pancake breakfast concluding the reunion on the Sunday following Labor Day weekend.

When we left Galesburg for College Park, Maryland, at the end of the summer of 1991, we chalked the small airport up as one of our secret things we'd miss.

As we discovered, though, College Park has its own small airport, one we found by wending our way around poorly designated roads in the tree cover off the Baltimore-Washington Parkway. Like the Galesburg Airport, Maryland's KCGS offers no commercial passenger flights. In fact, it appeared dinkier than Galesburg, with just one runway of 2980 feet tip to tip, no Jet-A fuel (though there is 100LL available), and a hand-drawn diagram of measurements for pilots wanting to land there.

To dismiss the College Park Airport, however, would be a huge mistake. KCGS is the oldest continuously operating airport in the world, up and running since 1909. Wilbur Wright of the first-flying Wright brothers trained our country's first military pilots at College Park. That same year, the first woman passenger took flight from this airfield. The first cross-country instrument-flight-rules (IFR) flight and the first US Postal Air Mail Service originated at College Park. It's the place of the first military mile-high flight (by Harold "Hap" Arnold, the US Air Force Commander during World War II), the first controlled helicopter flight, and the first testing of a machine gun on an aircraft. Arguably, this tiny airport is our nation's most historic airfield.

We visited the airport a couple of times for its annual air show, though the event seems to have disappeared. When we attended in the early 1990s, the air show featured a variety of aircraft on display and several flight demonstrations, including a wing-walker that made us gasp. We remember best a man restoring an old Boyd airplane made of corrugated metal, with household pipes for some of its parts. Such a project takes years, with much of the work painstaking in its detail. That day, he was taking out rivet after rivet in preparation for removing a rusted sheet of rippled wing.

By the late 1990s, we were exploring small airports elsewhere. To get to Rosecrans Memorial Airport, named for the sole hometown aviator to die during World War I, you have to cross Pony Express Bridge from St. Joseph, Missouri, and drive through a snippet of Kansas. The airfield has two runways, one of 8059 feet and the other spanning 4797 feet, and ninety-nine aircraft. The terminal was built in 1952, and under its control tower, which is open 8 a.m. to 6 p.m., is the worth-the-drive Airport Café, complete with large windows facing the runways and excellent breakfasts. For a small airport, it offers a lot of hubbub because the Missouri Air National Guard's 139th Air Lift Wing and its nine Hercules C-130s are based there.

On the West Coast, we frequented the Corvallis Municipal Airport, circling leisurely to catch a takeoff or landing from one of two runways. The city accepted the airfield from the US Army after World War II, and the latest records show more than 150 aircraft based there. Occasionally, we'd see fire-fighting helicopters practicing drills. Each small airport is a different incarnation.

When we returned to the College Park Airport last year, the airfield itself hadn't changed. But it was newly accessible down the street from the University of Maryland and boasted the College Park Aviation Museum, formerly dozens of small artifacts in a trailer and now an airy structure filled with old aircraft, memorabilia, and interactive exhibits. Some museum visitors must look out the vast window and wonder whether the asphalt in the midst of the overgrown grass is actually a runway. We imagine it bustling with the novelty of aviation a hundred years ago.

Field Notes from a New Terminal

Randy Malamud

It's simulation day at Atlanta's new Maynard H. Jackson Jr. International Terminal. Fifteen-hundred people with nothing better to do have volunteered to come down and try it out two weeks before opening day.

We've each been given "scripts" telling where we're supposed to "fly" and what we're supposed to do in the new terminal: go to the duty-free shops, find the SkyClub, locate the shuttle to Macon ("but don't get on the shuttle!" the script cautions).

My sons are good sports, and agree to come along with me. Jake has just finished his freshman year at Northeastern and has nothing better to do. Ben will miss a couple of his high-school classes.

We check in ("Volunteers are asked to bring at least two old suitcases, golf bags, garment bags, etc. with old clothes or towels inside to process through the new baggage system") for Delta flight "9754," to "Edinburgh," "leaving" at 10:00 and "arriving" at 10:05. At 10:15, we "return" to Atlanta, "arriving" at 10:30. Jake and I are ticketed in Business, but Ben's in Coach, which annoys him because he's actually a Silver Medallion and Jake's not.

At the counter, I try to get Ben upgraded, and the agent checks to see if he can arrange this ("Maybe I can do it for a fee," he says. "Dad, *please* don't pay real money for this," Ben whispers), but seems to forget about it before he has finished printing out our boarding passes. Here and elsewhere throughout the terminal, staff seem not quite sure how to handle the basics of check-in: no one can figure out exactly which gate our "flight" is supposed to leave from, for example. Good thing they're doing a dry run.

The new terminal is...completely adequate. The approach from the highway is futuristic-brutalist, efficient, sterile.

The façade features the glass and curves you'd expect.

It's not Schiphol or CDG or Eero Saarinen's TWA terminal; it doesn't aspire to be anything like those. It's just a tiny bit snazzy, with a couple of funky chandeliers, but nothing that would even mildly jostle middlebrow sensibilities.

It's like an entrée with one chili pepper at P.F. Chang's.

The ceilings undulate, as ceilings tend to do nowadays.

Inexplicably, the carpet pattern seems to be a parody of a seascape, with neurotically exaggerated waves.

The carpet tiles don't line up with each other, not even close. The bad visuals amplify the noxious new-carpet smell to create a generally nauseating effect.

The most appealing aspect of this terminal is that passengers are surrounded by runways in every direction, a prime attraction of any terminal—and, of course, something that's pretty hard to mess up in an airport design. There's a great view of my favorite Hartsfield icon: "FLY DELTA JETS." It's really the single colorful feature in ATL, the only thing in this massive compound that has any personality. When I see it, I know I'm home. (How long has it been since people called airplanes "jets"?)

Ben points out that the volunteers' demographics are surprisingly varied: "You'd think it would be all retired people." But there are old and young volunteers here, men and women, kids, toddlers. There's a woman in a powered wheelchair, apparently on her own, who seems to have considerable difficulty getting around—it surprises me that she signed up for what must be a difficult outing when she didn't actually have to go anywhere.

Which raises the question of why any of us are here. Most of us seem to be wondering that about all the others. Perhaps part of our motivation is public service: helping to get the bugs out of the system. Also, self-interest: learning how to navigate the new terminal in advance. The airline and airport employees seem very grateful to have us here; they bestow on everyone the gushing warmth that's usually reserved only for First Class passengers.

It's a little bit surreal seeing hundreds of "passengers" sitting around waiting for their "flights." There's the air of tedious impatience that always pervades waiting rooms, but obviously we've all *asked* to come here and wait, knowing that we wouldn't really be waiting for anything. So we can't complain.

We get to our gate and "board" — which means standing in the jetway for about ten minutes. After that, we're arriving passengers, and we file through to the customs and immigration hall. The lines there are long, and by this point most of the crowd, like us, seems to be over the novelty of it all.

The immigration officers are completely incompetent, even though they're not really processing arriving passengers. I don't know if they're pretending to be incompetent just to make this simulation seem realistic, or (more likely) that incompetence is simply their quidditas. It takes us an extra fifteen minutes here, because Jake's a smart-ass. As we're standing at the counter, a propos to nothing, he blurts out: "We brought back lots of agricultural diseases from Edinburgh." The officer looks up slowly, thinks about it for a couple of minutes, and calls over a supervisor. "How do you refer somebody," he asks? It takes him a while to figure it out (for future reference: type in "R"), and we get referred, and then another agent walks us through the hall, and checks and clears us. Our trip to nowhere ends a bit anti-climactically.

For those of us who spent the morning wandering around the airport without going anywhere, the simulation highlighted the aspects of airport transit that are pure routine and drudgery. Yet part of what's so compelling about this drudgery, paradoxically, is how intrinsically connected it is with the astounding phenomenon of flight and the fascination of travel. The dull bits provide a necessary counterpoint to all that: we enjoy the soaring adventure all the more because of the contrast with the security-line farce and the brutal skirmish to find outlets for recharging smartphones.

I love airports—I love moving through them and luxuriating in the mechanics of mobility. It's more fun, obviously, when I'm really going somewhere, but this pretend trip gave me the chance to think about what part of the experience comes simply from being at the airport. It's not a lot, but it's also not nothing. An okay time was had by all.

Vol de Nuit

Joanna Walsh

Please pay attention to the safety instructions, even if you are a frequent flyer.

I can't remember what the stewardess looked like, what kind of uniform she wore, whether she was young or old, pretty or not. I thought I would pay more attention because I am not a frequent flyer. For years I tried not to fly, didn't visit places that required it. It was not Green. It was also a kind of mental indulgence I didn't want to take. I didn't want to be the sort of person who thought some specific benefit came only with the very quickest change of scene, that I should go to other places to have particular kinds of experience, and, feeling displaced myself, I had no desire to treat other people as natives. For years I stuck to it, though I found it hard not to take flights when so many of the other people I knew who worried about taking flights, took them anyway. But here I am at an airport, hoping, just like them, that the most hopelessly non-specific meaning will take place.

I am about to cross a time zone, to lose another hour. *Night flight*, I am thinking, *Vol de Nuit*, which is a perfume by Guerlain that does not smell like this airport, which smells of the human props—coffee, cigarettes (for all that they're banned), cleaning fluids—that we use to keep ourselves, and our places, under control. Nor does the perfume smell of the mechanics of flight, of petrol and metal and the future seen from the narrow end of the twentieth century, like Caron's *Par Avion*, which is a perfume I like. It smells of being asleep, and flying at night is like being asleep: it is easier to let go of stolen hours (*vol*, in French, also means theft), or to pretend there were more of them. Night flight is nothing happening. It is a kind of denial.

It's a small world, and easy to cross if you have the time, and the money—from airport to airport at least, if those are the places where you want to arrive. Otherwise it can be a large world, and difficult to cross, difficult to find your way up a small track off the map once you leave the main road. But airport to airport is hardly travel. This airport looks like all the other airports I have been in. There is very little information here to tell me which country I am leaving and, when I arrive, it will be at a building very much like the one I have left. The airport is a buffer zone against loss of time and place. Specially designed to cushion the shocks of change, every corner is rounded, each surface easy to clean: plastic, marble, polished concrete. Against a background of undemanding grey, which suggests I might be in an office, functional fittings stand out in primary colors, hinting that I might be in a nursery, or on a building site. Shops that are open day and night breathe out a scent identical to fresh passionfruit, which, I know, comes from cosmetics and not from fruit at all. Signs threaten politely in every language: *Please do not leave your baggage unattended: it will be removed and destroyed*. The airport is made to run smoothly, so smoothly passengers slide off each other without a second glance. I go to the bar where sounds are submerged as in a swimming pool, which is decorated with chairs that imitate wood, upholstered in fabric that imitates flowering plants. I order a drink to celebrate being nowhere, after-hours. On the floorplan of the bar at the computerized till, island tables swim in a bright-blue sea.

Here in the airport it is easier to think of abstract things.

I am waiting for your reply to my email and I have settled into a waiting state, which is an airport state of mind. Waiting is familiar and its anxiety, once recognized, is comfortable. Loving is waiting for something to happen, even when I'm not always in the headlong state of being about to hear from you. The Internet, which is also so much waiting, doubles it. I can spend hours flicking from Twitter to Facebook to email, hypnotized, waiting for someone to make contact, to tell me I'm still here. I wait and

I don't do, until I find I have used up all my time, agreeably, waiting, until I almost feel I have done something. I could live in this suspended state (almost) indefinitely. Am I in love? Yes, since I am waiting, which is as much as to say, "Am I? Yes because I am waiting," which is as much as to say, "Am I? Yes because I am in love."

Waiting, I am carrying no extra weight. I have stripped myself to the bare minimum, even taken off my shoes and jacket to pass through security. I have moved my most intimate items—cosmetics, pills—to a plastic bag for inspection. Here in the airport—which is always warning me that I am too heavy, too large, too bulky, too liquid—I'm already pared-down to one bag, small enough for cabin luggage. But even now I am too much. I have to throw away a container of expensive face cream, too big for the carry-on regulations, which I regret. I have regretted nothing on my journey so far. I have pressed myself to test for regret, but I have not wanted to go back, have not thought I might have done better by acting differently but, now, as I stand over a bin by the x-ray machine, scraping the cream into a smaller container with a plastic teaspoon, jettisoning the rest, I regret that when my expensive cream runs out I will not be able to afford more. I regret that I will have to have none, or to make do with the kind of cheap cream from a supermarket that smells like fabric conditioner. Regret involves forward-thinking, a recognition of the consequences, an acceptance of loss. It feels like something to do with right and wrong because the emotion it brings up is almost exactly like guilt, or shame, though regret—especially for face cream—is not a moral feeling. It is strange that I feel regret only for such a small thing, and for a thing, which is not at all either good or bad.

Now I have started clearing myself out, I can't stop. I take everything from my bag that might weigh me down: receipts, screwed-up notes, a crumpled empty cigarette box. *Fumer nuit gravement à votre santé*, it tells me: *Smoking damages your health.*

Nuit. Vol de Nuit. Night flight. *Se nuire* (vb, French): to damage—
yourself or each other. A transitive, and a reflexive verb, you
can't do damage without damaging something, or someone.

I turn from the bin and into the corridor down the side of a
duty-free concession, thinking it leads to my gate but it ends in
an air-conditioning duct. A woman at the end of the corridor is
leaning on a trolley. On it there are many things in bags, so many,
and so full that I can't think how she got them through security,
but they are not bags for travelling: they are ragged and made of
plastic. She leans over her trolley, resting against it, as though
she has been pushing it for a long time. This airport that is so
bare and shiny is where she lives.

*All electronic devices must be switched off during take-off and
landing...*

In a row of three seats, I'm paired with a couple who, though
in their twenties, are playing top trumps with cards showing
puppets from a children's TV show. They will have to have learnt
so much about these fictional characters in order to play the
game. They are so into each other. They look only inward,
toward each other, one always half-turned in the other's
direction, her hand always on his arm, his fingers on her thigh.
When he takes off his cardigan it is her arm, not his, that reaches
around his shoulder to unbutton, and it looks like it should be
his, but unexpectedly white, short, and pointed, like a novelty
dance number where one partner stands behind the other,
invisible, doubling his number of limbs. When he eats crisps she
holds the bag and he feeds first himself, and then her. They have
no in independent action. Her face is pale and unformed. He
pushes up the thick black scaffold of glasses to kiss her, and
underneath her face is helpless as a slug.

The stewardesses offer headsets for a small fee, and the
passengers pay to quiet themselves. Because they have spent
money, they agree that silence is necessary. The headphones link
to a playlist, but there's nothing else to entertain us on this flight,

which is too short for love or for action, at least the way they tell it in the movies. Instead I fall asleep and dream that I am dead. *I am still on earth with other dead people waiting to be passed on to somewhere else. By a kind of customs desk, I wait with my ex brother-in-law. We discuss comic books we have read — now we are waiting, we will have time to catch up on our reading. I ask the customs officer whether it is possible for the dead to fall in love. He looks regretful. He says, definitely, "No."* I open my eyes to find large tears burning down opposite sides of my face into the airline pillow.

A hostess nudges me awake: drink? biscuits? Although I do not want the drink, and do not like the biscuits, I eat them because they are given, and drink warm white wine from a tiny plastic bottle. We fly over places I have seen named in IKEA catalogues. I never thought to pry them off the page. I cross a little boundary on the map into the shaded part of the world, where alcohol leaks in to loosen up the mind, to let stories out. Words hang in front of me as on the runway, illuminated: I cannot say them, I have no one to say them to. In the seats in front of me, an old man and an old woman don't know each other. They find the words that come out are to do with their grown-up children. Deal, play, trump: it's difficult for me to listen. I have planned for nothing beyond the hotel at the end of my flight, but I'm buoyed up by faith in other people's plans, as the plane is buoyed up because the passengers believe it is flying and, if we stop believing, it will fall. The old people talk in operatic vistas: friends, relatives marry, divorce, die, all in a sentence. Everything happens to everyone; it's no surprise. So much is concluded. Their stories have ends, and people come to them, even before the fasten-seatbelts sign goes off. I listen like I might learn something: they have been stocking their memories for so long, long enough, perhaps, for them to begin to see a pattern. Storytelling is a consequence of survival and each tale — told as though it could have happened only that way — irons out regret. But they don't foresee their own ends, not these old people who are really not that old—in their sixties maybe. Like children they still haven't learned that things will go on beyond them.

Turbulence: people fasten their seatbelts with the sound of bubble-wrap popping. Things shake and fall from the overhead lockers, as though there were a right-way-up, as though the plane were a house set on solid ground that could be pushed off balance. The chicken-leg wheels descend from the plane's under-carriage. *Take nothing with you.* If we go down, metal stripping from the aircraft roof, if we gallop though the houses at double speed...but I've always had a problem with the might-have-been. As it is, after an interval of unsure minutes the uncrushed plane leaves a shadow of its crash across the rooftops, across desire.

Flight Benefits

Tony D'Souza

My mother worked reservations at United Airlines in Chicago before all those jobs were sent to India, and, not having any clue how fortunate I was, I grew up on planes. I have no idea how many millions of free miles I flew, but I did manage to visit fifty countries by the time my benefits ran out when I turned twenty-five.

It was an odd experience for a kid from a middle-income family; while everyone else in our neighborhood was lucky to hit the skies to Disney or Cancun once a year, I could fly whenever I wanted. My parents started letting me take daytrips alone when I was fifteen. I remember flying to St. Louis just to buy a rare comic book. Another time a neighbor paid me $150 to fly to Portland and bring back an exotic breed of cat for her.

So much has changed about air travel; I remember when flying was a luxury experience, when the flight attendants were nice to you and everyone got a meal. Today, it's as rough as hitchhiking and the planes are all beat to hell.

What I loved best was flying internationally, mostly because once you left the States, nobody cared how old you were, and there was always free booze on the planes and in the international lounges. I used to always get really drunk in those lounges. The best time was when I had a layover in Tokyo on my way to India in 1993. I was eighteen, I ended up drinking seven or eight Asahis with some business traveler from Houston wearing a cowboy hat. By the time I checked the boards for my flight to Singapore, I saw that I'd missed it. Missing a flight is no cause for concern when you fly for free; you simply hop the next one. Unfortunately, there was no next flight to Singapore that day.

I asked the Japanese United agents what I should do and they said I should spend the night in Tokyo. Fine, I said, but how much would that cost? Well, they said, Tokyo is very expensive. I might find a room for $200. Since that was almost half the cash I had, I shook my head and asked what else I could do. They said there was a last flight to Hong Kong, which was cheaper than Japan, so I hopped it.

My memory is pretty vague about what happened next, but I do remember drinking a couple vodkas on the plane, and later being helped up off the gritty airport floor by some Chinese soldiers, in British uniforms, carrying sub-machines guns. Then my passport was stamped; I know this because I still have that old passport with the stamp in it. Then I was in a cab, and somehow in a tiny room on a high floor of a beat-up hotel looking down at the lights of Victoria Harbor. There were a couple of dreadlocked French guys in the room with me smoking hash. I'm not sure how they got there. Then I was in a bar where a white chick was belly-dancing for all these Asian businessmen. When I tried to talk to her, she was Russian. I guess I said the wrong thing, because I got karate-chopped in the stomach by someone and thrown out.

Anyway, I ended up winning this dart contest in a British pub and met this Hungarian girl and we spent a few days shacked up in her filthy little Hong Kong tenement. Why a chick who could pass for American had to live as low as that, I didn't understand, but I didn't know about the conditions of Eastern Europe at that time. I just thought it was really romantic. She was a nanny for an English family, and we mostly spoke in pantomime. I'd lost my bag because I couldn't remember the name of the first hotel, so I wore an *I Love Hong Kong* T-shirt I bought from a street vendor, plus some cheap sunglasses. But I had my passport and a few travelers' checks. Me and the Hungarian had a fight about something and she kicked me out, so I went to the only safe place I knew: the airport.

All the flights out of Hong Kong were packed, so I got stuck sleeping in that airport for two nights. Then I got to Singapore and spent two weeks there trying to get to India because the flights were all full. One of the weeks I spent hunkered in the airport, trying to get on flight after flight and living on crackers and butter that I kept stealing from a sandwich shop. It wasn't as bad as that Iranian who lived in Charles de Gaulle airport for eighteen years, but it was shitty enough. International airports are cool when you're just passing through, all duty-free cigarettes and hot chicks from everywhere. But when you're trapped in one, it's the worst sort of purgatory. There's nowhere to clean up in any decent way. A few hours of the stress of being stuck, coupled with the benches designed to keep you from getting comfortable, and pretty soon you look like what you are for the moment: homeless. The second week I stopped trying the daytime flights, instead took the bus into downtown Singapore, walking along glitzy Orchard Road where I couldn't afford to buy anything, and melting in the heat as I ate greasy noodles in cheap basement chop shops packed with Filipino laborers.

Finally, I made it to India after having to do something I never had before: buying a ticket. This was on India Airways and the plane had metal plates riveted to the fuselage so it looked like a motley quilt-work of patches, and the cabin was filled with fog. The flight attendants in saris ladled curry into bowls that people brought with them for the meal. It was like being in the bowels of a cargo ship; pretty much what flying in the States is like today.

I would travel like that, saving up just enough money at home cutting lawns and selling pot to let me live in the Third World cheaply for months. Then when my flight benefits ran out, I immediately joined the Peace Corps, which got me over to Africa for three years. I love to fly, still get a giddy feeling each and every time I board a plane, even if I try to look as experienced as all the snooty Business Class travelers lining up to walk over the tiny and ridiculous red carpet. I used to like talking to strangers on planes, but not anymore. The rest of it is the same for me to this day, the plane lifting up, your body feeling strange, the earth receding and receding until it all just has to be a dream. Anything still feels possible for that one moment.

Concourse B

Jane Armstrong

Every flight is a continuation of the same flight.

The airplane photo: 1963. Me, a little girl, blond hair curled specially, Sunday-best dress, ruffled socks under patent-leather Mary Janes, white gloves (yes, gloves!), sitting in a first-class seat so big that my outstretched legs do not reach the edge of the seat cushion. My mother sits next to me in the window seat, smiling frosted-orange for the camera. She, too, is suitably turned out in a smartly tailored dress with matching hat. We are flying north to visit living ancestors, wealthy people of property. "Only the very elite flew back then," my mother will say, years later, when we are far from elite.

Annually, for decades, I fly transcontinentally to visit my mother as she ages.

Waiting at Gate 17, Concourse B, I am unburdened by personal history. I don't have to be the poor daughter of the only divorced mother in my school. On Concourse B, I am defined by my carefully chosen costume and the demeanor I adopt to fit it. I pose as a woman of means traveling alone, outfitted in a semi-nautical blue linen jacket, white silk blouse, high-end jeans, comfortable but expensive ballet flats, all casually thrown together—a look I appropriated from fashion magazines and celebrity spy shots. I maintain a sight line slightly above or to the side of the other passengers. Jackie O sans sunglasses.

"Did they give you something good to eat on the plane?" This is always the first thing my mother asks after the hello-darling kisses and hugs. She rarely waits for an answer. She wants to tell me, year after year, about the sumptuous fare we were served on that one special flight— the juicy filet mignon with herbed potatoes, seasoned and cooked to perfection and presented on real china with silver-plated flatware on a linen placemat. And then the dessert, the best ice cream she ever had, garnished with fresh raspberries and a sprig of fresh mint. When I tell her airlines don't serve food like that anymore, she says, "It's just like a bus now, a cattle car. I can't be bothered." She says this instead of "I can't afford to travel."

On my thirty-second trip, a hospice nurse whispers that my mother is "not expected to live." I climb into my mother's bed and curl myself against blanketed bones. She strokes my head and says, "It's all right, darling, it's all right," like I'm the little girl with shiny shoes on the airplane seat, terrified when the plane takes off.

Although located at precise coordinates, the airport, like a doctor's office waiting room or a nursing home, exists nowhere-in-particular. Touches of local color fail to ground. Timepieces are mounted everywhere—schedules of arrivals and departures, gate-desk monitors, stand-by update displays—but, paradoxically, time itself stretches and warps, holding the passenger in eternal present.

For trip thirty-three, I book First Class. The seat will be spacious and comfortable and I will be given a hot hand towel in preparation for the special meal I will eat with real flatware (not silver plate, but not plastic either). I'll have a catalogue of movies to choose from on my own private screen and I'll get whatever I want to drink with the snacks that will keep coming for hours and hours. Amidst the front-of-the-plane amenities, I will pretend to be the great lady my mother had hoped to be. I am not anxious to board. My mother will not be at my destination to ask about the flight, to say that it sounds nice, but not nearly as wonderful as the only plane trip we took together.

Time moves predictably one second per second, except on Concourse B. I am content to stay here, in this timeless non-place, where flight is perpetually delayed and the airplane photo, 1963, is never moved from the nightstand next to the empty bed.

Acknowledgements & Credits

The editors would like to thank the English Department and the Dean's Office of the College of Arts and Sciences of Loyola University New Orleans for supporting our project. A special thank you to our student researchers: Erin Little, Elizabeth Nellams, Dustin O'Keefe Poelker, Julia del Rivero, and Stewart Sinclair. Thanks to Susan Clements for indexing and to Nancy Bernardo for her cover art.

Thank you to our families for putting up with this obsession.

"The Doctor's Wife" by Anya Groner was adapted for the *New York Times'* Modern Love Column under the title "Is There a Doctor in the Marriage?"

"Holding Pattern," from Ander Monson's *Letter to a Future Lover*, is reprinted here with the permission of The Permissions Company, Inc. on behalf of Graywolf Press, Minneapolis, Minnesota.

"Hostages (October 23–24, 1975)" by Allison Kinney was first published in the Unpalatable Issue of Project As[I]Am.

Index

Page references for illustrations appear in *italics*

Contemporary culture has eliminated both the concept of the public and the figure of the intellectual. Former public spaces – both physical and cultural – are now either derelict or colonized by advertising. A cretinous anti-intellectualism presides, cheerled by expensively educated hacks in the pay of multinational corporations who reassure their bored readers that there is no need to rouse themselves from their interpassive stupor. The informal censorship internalized and propagated by the cultural workers of late capitalism generates a banal conformity that the propaganda chiefs of Stalinism could only ever have dreamt of imposing. Zer0 Books knows that another kind of discourse – intellectual without being academic, popular without being populist – is not only possible: it is already flourishing, in the regions beyond the striplit malls of so-called mass media and the neurotically bureaucratic halls of the academy. Zer0 is committed to the idea of publishing as a making public of the intellectual. It is convinced that in the unthinking, blandly consensual culture in which we live, critical and engaged theoretical reflection is more important than ever before.

ZERO BOOKS

Capitalist Realism Is there no alternative?
Mark Fisher
An analysis of the ways in which capitalism has presented itself as the only realistic political-economic system.
Paperback: November 27, 2009 978-1-84694-317-1 $14.95 £7.99.
eBook: July 1, 2012 978-1-78099-734-6 $9.99 £6.99.

The Wandering Who? A study of Jewish identity politics
Gilad Atzmon
An explosive unique crucial book tackling the issues of Jewish Identity Politics and ideology and their global influence.
Paperback: September 30, 2011 978-1-84694-875-6 $14.95 £8.99.
eBook: September 30, 2011 978-1-84694-876-3 $9.99 £6.99.

Clampdown Pop-cultural wars on class and gender
Rhian E. Jones
Class and gender in Britpop and after, and why 'chav' is a feminist issue.
Paperback: March 29, 2013 978-1-78099-708-7 $14.95 £9.99.
eBook: March 29, 2013 978-1-78099-707-0 $7.99 £4.99.

The Quadruple Object
Graham Harman
Uses a pack of playing cards to present Harman's metaphysical system of fourfold objects, including human access, Heidegger's indirect causation, panpsychism and ontography.
Paperback: July 29, 2011 978-1-84694-700-1 $16.95 £9.99.

Weird Realism Lovecraft and Philosophy
Graham Harman
As Hölderlin was to Martin Heidegger and Mallarmé to Jacques
Derrida, so is H.P. Lovecraft to the Speculative Realist philoso-
phers.
Paperback: September 28, 2012 978-1-78099-252-5 $24.95 £14.99.
eBook: September 28, 2012 978-1-78099-907-4 $9.99 £6.99.

Sweetening the Pill or How We Got Hooked on Hormonal Birth
Control
Holly Grigg-Spall
Is it really true? Has contraception liberated or oppressed
women?
Paperback: September 27, 2013 978-1-78099-607-3 $22.95 £12.99.
eBook: September 27, 2013 978-1-78099-608-0 $9.99 £6.99.

Why Are We The Good Guys? Reclaiming Your Mind From The
Delusions Of Propaganda
David Cromwell
A provocative challenge to the standard ideology that Western
power is a benevolent force in the world.
Paperback: September 28, 2012 978-1-78099-365-2 $26.95 £15.99.
eBook: September 28, 2012 978-1-78099-366-9 $9.99 £6.99.

The Truth about Art Reclaiming quality
Patrick Doorly
The book traces the multiple meanings of art to their various
sources, and equips the reader to choose between them.
Paperback: August 30, 2013 978-1-78099-841-1 $32.95 £19.99.

Bells and Whistles More Speculative Realism
Graham Harman
In this diverse collection of sixteen essays, lectures, and inter-
views Graham Harman lucidly explains the principles of

Speculative Realism, including his own object-oriented philosophy.
Paperback: November 29, 2013 978-1-78279-038-9 $26.95 £15.99.
eBook: November 29, 2013 978-1-78279-037-2 $9.99 £6.99.

Towards Speculative Realism: Essays and Lectures Essays and Lectures
Graham Harman
These writings chart Harman's rise from Chicago sportswriter to co founder of one of Europe's most promising philosophical movements: Speculative Realism.
Paperback: November 26, 2010 978-1-84694-394-2 $16.95 £9.99.
eBook: January 1, 1970 978-1-84694-603-5 $9.99 £6.99.

Meat Market Female flesh under capitalism
Laurie Penny
A feminist dissection of women's bodies as the fleshy fulcrum of capitalist cannibalism, whereby women are both consumers and consumed.
Paperback: April 29, 2011 978-1-84694-521-2 $12.95 £6.99.
eBook: May 21, 2012 978-1-84694-782-7 $9.99 £6.99.

Translating Anarchy The Anarchism of Occupy Wall Street
Mark Bray
An insider's account of the anarchists who ignited Occupy Wall Street.
Paperback: September 27, 2013 978-1-78279-126-3 $26.95 £15.99.
eBook: September 27, 2013 978-1-78279-125-6 $6.99 £4.99.

One Dimensional Woman
Nina Power
Exposes the dark heart of contemporary cultural life by examining pornography, consumer capitalism and the ideology of women's work.

Paperback: November 27, 2009 978-1-84694-241-9 $14.95 £7.99.
eBook: July 1, 2012 978-1-78099-737-7 $9.99 £6.99.

Dead Man Working
Carl Cederstrom, Peter Fleming
An analysis of the dead man working and the way in which capital is now colonizing life itself.
Paperback: May 25, 2012 978-1-78099-156-6 $14.95 £9.99.
eBook: June 27, 2012 978-1-78099-157-3 $9.99 £6.99.

Unpatriotic History of the Second World War
James Heartfield
The Second World War was not the Good War of legend. James Heartfield explains that both Allies and Axis powers fought for the same goals - territory, markets and natural resources.
Paperback: September 28, 2012 978-1-78099-378-2 $42.95 £23.99.
eBook: September 28, 2012 978-1-78099-379-9 $9.99 £6.99.

Find more titles at www.zero-books.net